Bilingual Education in Massachusetts

The Emperor Has No Clothes

Bilingual Education in Massachusetts

The Emperor Has No Clothes

Christine H. Rossell

and

Keith Baker

Pioneer Institute
Boston, Massachusetts

Cover Art: Ralph Buglass, Winchester, Massachusetts
Printing: Pitney Bowes, Stamford, Connecticut
Desktop Publishing: OMNI/OfficePlus, Boston, Massachusetts and WordSmith, Rockland, Massachusetts

Library of Congress Cataloging-in-Publication Data

Rossell, Christine H.
Bilingual education in Massachusetts : the emperor has no clothes /Christine H. Rossell and Keith Baker.
p. cm. -- (Pioneer paper : no. 10)
Includes bibliographical references and index.
ISBN 0-929930-14-2
1. Education, Bilingual--Massachusetts. 2. Education and state--Massachusetts. 3. Linguistic minorities--Education--Massachusetts. I. Baker, Keith. II. Title. III. Series.
LC3732.M4R68 1996
371.97'009744--dc20 96-2788
CIP

Pioneer Institute for Public Policy Research

Pioneer Institute is a public policy research organization that specializes in the support, distribution, and promotion of scholarly research on Massachusetts public policy issues. Its main program—the Pioneer Paper series—consists of research projects commissioned from area scholars. The Institute publishes these papers and communicates the research results to decision makers in government and opinion leaders in business, academia, and the media. Pioneer Institute is supported by corporate, foundation, and individual contributions and qualifies under IRS rules for 501 (c)(3) tax-exempt status.

Pioneer Institute recognizes the generous support of its members. It is only with your support—financial and otherwise—that Pioneer can continue to publish studies and sponsor forums.

To teachers—without whom there would be no literacy in any language.

TABLE OF CONTENTS

Foreword

The enactment of the Massachusetts Transitional Bilingual Education Act, in 1971, was a triumph of good intentions and generous sentiments. Then in my first year as the state official responsible for urban education and equity, and thus "present at the creation," I can remember vividly what we hoped and expected from this first-in-the-nation legislation.

Sister Francis Georgia Vicente, a Franciscan nun, had gone from door to door in the South End, the previous year, discovering that hundreds of Puerto Rican children were not in school at all. Mona Hull of the Advent School, working through St. Stephen's Episcopal Church, had tested dozens of Hispanic children in public school special education classes and found that their only problem was not understanding the language used in regular classrooms. And "ethnic heritage" was on everyone's lips; if Black was Beautiful, why shouldn't others feel pride in their ethnicity and seek to affirm and maintain it?

All of this was bubbling when Sister Francis Georgia and others lobbied through a bill drafted by lawyers at Harvard. There was from the start, however, a confusion of purposes that has bedeviled bilingual education in Massachusetts ever since. Was this a program about teaching languages other than English? My colleague at the Massachusetts Department of Education, Ernest Mazzone, was supervisor for foreign languages and served as a liaison to the drafting process. Or was it about overcoming the barriers that divided (and still divide!) many Hispanic and other language minority children from successful participation in our educational system and society? In that case, it would fall within my jurisdiction.

For Commissioner of Education Neil V. Sullivan, a veteran of the civil rights battles, it was clear that the new law should be a vehicle for effective integration and equal opportunity, so he gave me responsibility for it; Ernest Mazzone took a job as foreign language director in Haverhill. Writing the Commissioner's testimony in support of the bilingual bill, I took care to acknowledge the dignity and value of the languages with which children come to school. A teenager coming from Portugal should be able to continue to learn history or algebra in Portuguese while learning English. "This bill reminds us," I wrote, "that it is possible to be intelligent and wise, learned and thoughtful, in many languages!" But equity was the bottom line.

In effect, our intention was to use the new bilingual education law in close conjunction with another of our legislative priorities enacted in 1971, the Anti-Discrimination Law (Chapter 622), and with the Racial Imbalance Law (1965) to push for the full participation of language minority children in Massachusetts schools. It was not to create a separate and imperfectly parallel educational track for them. Segregation of minority children, we thought then and I remain convinced today, was what we should be seeking to overcome.

The early seventies were a time when government was constantly creating new programs for ever-more-closely-defined groups of students and seeking to protect these programs from the presumed indifference or hostility of the regular education system by setting up separate lines of authority. The new law devoted nearly 500 words to defining a new bureau, reporting directly to the Commissioner—the clear intent was to insulate implementation of this program from the other objectives of the department. After about a year of letting me use the law as part of a general strategy for improving the education of minority children, Commissioner Sullivan capitulated and set up the new bureau, with Mazzone coming back to direct it. From that point on, bilingual education went its separate way as a language-and-culture program.

Sister Francis Georgia came to work for me, with a roving license to ensure that bilingual programs operated in the interest of poor children, and we obtained federal funding to set up a team charged with enforcing the civil rights protections related to national origin and, later, refugees. But we were repeatedly frustrated in our efforts to hold bilingual programs accountable for measurable outcomes. Our colleagues in the bilingual bureau would not (as the law required) prescribe an annual test of English proficiency and successfully resisted inclusion of bilingual program pupils in the statewide assessments, and any limit on number of years in the program.

So much for the sad history of a generous reform that has not produced the successful participation we had hoped for. The experience of other Western democracies with the education of immigrant children helps to illuminate what went wrong. In France and Germany, Australia and Canada, Belgium and the Netherlands, Denmark and Switzerland, education authorities have responded to the influx of children from families who don't speak the national language(s) by implementing two sorts of programs, often serving the same pupils but with different purposes which our bilingual programs seek unsuccessfully to combine.

Reception classes are widely used for children who arrive after the age when children start school. For a year and in exceptional cases for two, the language of the school is taught in a concentrated way, together with more general instruction on how to get along in the host society and its schools. For older children in particular, previous academic work in the homeland is assessed to make the best placement in classes that will continue what they have already learned. Some of the better programs also have each child spend part of each day from the start with the class into which he or she will eventually be integrated, to begin to form relationships and feel at home. Accountability for results are fundamental to this approach, as it has not been for transitional bilingual education in Massachusetts.

These educational systems also commonly provide supplemental classes, sometimes after school and sometimes during elective periods in the school day, to develop and maintain the home language of immigrant children. The home language is seen as a valuable asset that should, if possible, not be lost. These classes are voluntary and quite popular, though the level of participation varies among ethnic groups, as the data on parent attitudes in the United States would suggest.

The strategy, in brief, is to integrate immigrant children as quickly as possible and then support their continuing to be competent—if they so choose—in the language of their heritage. These programs do not always work well, of course, but the fundamental approach seems sounder than our own. In transitional bilingual education we seek to integrate children while educating them separately, we seek to build upon their home language while dropping its use and development as soon as they are judged capable of doing schoolwork in English, we seek to make them educationally successful while not daring to ask them to take the standardized tests by which we measure the progress of other pupils. Our approach is self-contradictory and fails many children; if it works well for some, that is more by happy accident than by design.

The kindness of our bilingual program—and I repeat that it was most generously conceived—has been most unkind in its working out. Christine Rossell and Keith Baker have put us in their debt by bringing together in an unusually scrupulous way the research evidence on achievement in bilingual programs. If they have not been able to shed much light on the actual results produced by bilingual education in Massachusetts, or its costs, that is because (for reasons suggested above) the program was long run by the state in a manner that discouraged accountability for outcomes while being strict about procedural compliance: a program would be censured for failing to translate a routine notice into Khmer, but not asked whether Cambodian pupils were going on to success in high school.

What emerges with greatest clarity from Rossell and Baker's study is the extreme diversity of programs that exist under the label of bilingual education, and thus the impossibility of reaching any general conclusion about their value. Advocacy of bilingual education—and I consider myself an advocate, and have put five of my own children in a bilingual school in Boston—remains an act of faith. Certainly it provides a rich education to those children who are fortunate enough to be in well-run programs with well-trained teachers, well-integrated with their schools. Undoubtedly it provides a miserable education to other children, the "educational dead-end" against which the Supreme Court warned in the *Lau* decision. Surely we must do better to ensure that no language minority child is educationally segregated by the failure of our good intentions.

What would I propose instead? Better than our present cul-de-sac would be a double strategy of effective reception programs stressing English followed by speedy integration and continuing voluntary support of home language development and use. Of course, as Rossell and Baker show, some so-called "bilingual" programs (especially for Asian pupils) actually teach only English and mainstream quite quickly, though without offering the opportunity available to language minority children in other countries, to continue to develop their home language to become truly bilingual.

Best of all would be for 200 (charter?) schools across the Commonwealth to become consistently bilingual, with voluntary enrollment of English-dominant pupils and pupils dominant in the second language of the school. A bilingual school would have a principal well versed in language development and a number of teachers proficient in its target language; together they would make it their business to ensure that every pupil had a rich educational experience incorporating both languages in an effective way, avoiding segregation on the one side and frustration on the other. Homerooms would be integrated, pupils would be separated by dominant language only for short-term activities, all would be expected to achieve academically, those from English-speaking families would have the opportunity to acquire some proficiency in another language, and those from families who speak another language would be exposed to colloquial as well as academic English as a matter of course.

Charles L. Glenn
April 1996

***

Charles L. Glenn is Professor of Educational Policy at Boston University. His latest book (with Ester de Jong) is *Educating Immigrant Children: A Comparative Study of 12 Countries*, New York: Garland, 1996.

Acknowledgments

Needless to say, a book of this length and complexity cannot be written without the help and cooperation of hundreds of individuals in federal, state, and local government and the academy. We are indebted to all the individuals who provided us with countless hours of explanation of bilingual education legislation and regulations, who gave us reports and documents often free of charge, who really wanted us to understand this complex subject. There were several people in the Massachusetts state government who provided us with the TBE reports, with documents describing teacher certification, letters sent to school districts, and the Executive Office of Education survey. These people continued to answer follow-up call after call over the months and years that it took to research and write this book. No one ever refused to talk to us and no one was ever anything less than knowledgeable and candid. We have no doubt that the people who run our state and local governments, with only a few exceptions, are the finest individuals in our society. Unfortunately, as James Q. Wilson's book *Bureaucracy* discusses, these competent, hardworking individuals work within a set of constraints imposed by the taxpayers and their representatives in the legislature that would cause paralysis in most private companies. That our governments at all levels continue to work at all is a tribute to the outstanding women and men who staff it.

Chapter 4 of this book could not have been written without the openness, patience, and candor of all the school district staff, principals, and bilingual education teachers who allowed Christine Rossell to traipse through their schools and classrooms and who spent hundreds of hours explaining what it is they do. Only two principals turned Rossell down and no teacher did. The bilingual education teachers were proud of their teaching abilities and they deserve to be. Regardless of the language they taught in, they were enthusiastic and caring and dedicated to helping their students become successful and productive citizens. They were willing to be observed at any time by anyone. Indeed, this is typical of the candor and openness of American public servants that makes American government the most open and responsive in the world, as Wilson also points out in his book.

We are grateful to the reviewers of this book, Charles Glenn, Diane Ravitch, Chester Finn, Russell Fleming, Jeffrey Miron, Nathan Glazer, Rosalie Porter, William Edgerly, Tom McDermott, Nicolás Sánchez, Jorge Amselle, and Bruce Cooper, who obviously read it carefully because they made numerous, insightful comments and, as a result, improved the book enormously.

We are indebted to the staff of Pioneer Institute for their patience and editorial assistance throughout the years this project took. Steven Wilson and Virginia Straus first approached us three years ago and helped get the project off the ground with their ideas and insights. Over the last two years, Gabriela Mrad and Jim Peyser provided editorial assistance, advice, materials, and support that made this book a reality. In particular, Gabriela's persistent prodding and intelligent and caring advice must be credited with the fact that we finally completed this task that we began almost three years ago. Kathryn Ciffolillo turned our sometimes turgid prose into understandable English and caught numerous contradictions, repetitions, and instances of illogic. In short, she provided the very best kind of editing—she improved both the style and the substance of the writing of two researchers who are still struggling with the English language, despite the fact that it is our native tongue. However, as the experts in this field, we must take ultimate responsibility for any mistakes.

We are indebted to the Pioneer Institute and its donors for funding the research and writing of this book and for their patience over the years that it took to complete the project. We are also grateful to our families, including Smudge, who put up with the hours that this project took from our family life.

We would like to thank our research assistants, Jasmin Daze, Nina Nguyen and Andrés Alvarez for their help in constructing charts and tables, conducting research and retrieving documents.

We are grateful to all the immigrants who have come to our shores, including our own ancestors who had to struggle with the English language. We admit to being hopeless romantics on the subject of immigration. We believe that our immigrants are the greatest resource this country has and the reason the topic of bilingual education is so important. Finally, as noted in the dedication to this book, we are grateful to teachers without whom there would be no literacy in any language.

CHAPTER ONE

INTRODUCTION AND SUMMARY

Massachusetts is one of only nine states in the country to require bilingual education in all school districts where there is a sufficient number of limited-English-proficient (LEP) students. Moreover, Massachusetts has set the lowest threshold for mandatory bilingual education in the country: 20 LEP students in a single language group in a district—an average of fewer than 2 students in each grade—triggers native tongue instruction in a separate classroom taught by a bilingual certified teacher. In total, almost 40,000 students in 51 Massachusetts districts were enrolled in bilingual education programs in 1993-94. Nevertheless, observations of actual classroom practice demonstrate that these students are not all receiving the same style of education. As a general rule, only Spanish-speaking students—who comprise more than half of the LEP population in the Commonwealth—are taught to read and write in their native language, while also receiving some native language instruction in other academic subjects, as existing law requires. Students from virtually all other language groups, though enrolled in "bilingual education," receive instruction almost exclusively in English, with at most a few hours per week of enrichment in their native languages and cultures. By way of example, many of these students are taught primarily in regular education classrooms and are pulled out for instruction in English as a Second Language (ESL). Even some Spanish-speaking LEP students in "bilingual education" are not taught to read or write in their native language.

The diversity of practice becomes even more apparent when one takes into account the differences between elementary and secondary grades. At the elementary level, there is at least a chance that a district might be able to pull together enough students in the same language group to fill a bilingual education class, with its own certified teacher who is fluent in both English and the applicable foreign language. At the secondary level, however, where most students move from one classroom and one subject to another throughout the school day, it is next to impossible to assemble a large enough teaching staff to ensure that each LEP student receives instruction in his or her native language. The extent of native language instruction is further influenced by the language skills of individual teachers (who are currently not required to be fluent in English) and the availability of foreign language texts and materials applicable to the curriculum. In sum, it is not unusual to find great differences in educational programs for LEP students from one language to another, from one district to another, from one grade to another, and even from one classroom to another.

One would expect the spotty implementation of the Massachusetts bilingual education law to be cause for complaint. In reality, however, it has been the flexible implementation (or non-implementation) of this rather prescriptive law that has kept the program from collapsing of its own weight. Twenty-five years after passage of the bilingual education law in Massachusetts, there is still no evidence to prove that the mandated approach to teaching works better than other approaches, such as intensive English instruction. Not only is there no evidence from Massachusetts, but there is no evidence from the many studies that have been conducted in other states. Indeed, if one can draw any conclusion at all from the research it is that teaching a LEP student to read and write in the native language is at least marginally detrimental to his or her overall education and acquisition of English. While test scores and high school completion rates among Hispanic students in

Massachusetts (a significant portion of whom are or have been in TBE programs) have improved over the past 25 years, they have fallen relative to other groups since enactment of the Transitional Bilingual Education Act in 1971. At a minimum, the program has not fulfilled the expectations of its supporters.

Because of these findings we recommend that the existing mandate to provide bilingual programs be amended to require that districts simply provide "educational programs" targeted to LEP children. Of equal importance, the impractical threshold of 20 LEP students in a single language group in a district should be relaxed. Furthermore, the law should be amended to require teachers of LEP children to demonstrate fluency in English and to allow placement of students in separate LEP classrooms only with the express and prior consent of their parents.

Alternative Approaches to Educating LEP Students

Bilingual education,[1] as it is commonly called, is a controversial issue throughout Massachusetts and the United States. At the heart of this controversy are three issues: 1) Should LEP children receive, because of their language barrier, special instruction not given to other children with learning problems? 2) Should LEP children be taught to read and write in their native language? and 3) Should time be taken out of the regular instructional day to teach LEP children about their particular culture? Although the public may disagree about the answers to these questions, federal and state policymakers have, since 1968 in the United States and 1971 in Massachusetts, come squarely down on the affirmative side. Both the federal government and the state of Massachusetts have provided billions of dollars to fund programs that provide instruction in the native language and in the native culture of LEP children.

The national literature acknowledges four basic instructional alternatives for teaching LEP children. The first of the models is submersion, often called "sink-or-swim." In this model, the LEP child is placed in a regular English-language classroom with monolingual children and given no more special help than any child with educational problems.

A second technique is English as a Second Language (ESL) instruction for one or two periods a day, or in some districts two or three periods a week, and participation in the regular English-language classroom for the rest of the time. ESL is a pullout program usually based on a special curriculum for teaching English to LEP children, but the instructors do not have to speak the child's native language.

A third instructional technique is structured immersion—instruction is in the second language being learned (English) in a self-contained classroom, but the teacher usually knows how to speak the students' native language. Instruction is geared to the children's language proficiency at each stage so that it is comprehensible; students thus learn the second language and subject matter content simultaneously. The native language is used only in the rare instances when a child cannot complete a task without it. In the United States, the term "structured immersion" is almost never used by practitioners. Teachers and administrators call such programs "bilingual education," "bilingual immersion,"[2] or, particularly at the secondary level, "sheltered" classes—for example, "Sheltered English I," "Sheltered English II," and so forth.

The fourth instructional technique is transitional bilingual education (TBE).[3] In TBE, the student is taught to read and write in the native language, with subject matter also taught in the native language.

The second language (i.e., English) is initially taught for only a small portion of the day. As the child progresses in English, the amount of instructional time in the native language is reduced and English increased until the student is proficient enough in English to join the regular instructional program. This transition is typically made over a three-year period. The rationale underlying TBE differs depending on the age of the child. For very young children, it is that learning to read in the native language first is a necessary condition for optimal reading ability in the second language. For all children, regardless of age, it is also argued that learning a second language takes time and children should not lose ground in other subject matters, particularly math, during that period. The educational theory used to explain how TBE works is known as the facilitation theory. First presented by James Cummins in 1978, this theory has two parts: the first states that in order to make optimal cognitive progress in a second language, a LEP child must first attain a "threshold" level of competence in the native language. The second part attributes to native language skills a facilitating effect on learning the grammar and usage of a second language. Of the four methods, only TBE is characterized by instruction to develop literacy in the native (i.e., non-English) language.

A variation on transitional bilingual education is bilingual maintenance.[4] These programs resemble TBE in their early years, but they differ in that their goal is to produce fully bilingual children, and thus students do not leave when they master English.

Bilingual Education in Massachusetts

The Transitional Bilingual Education Act, Chapter 71A of the Massachusetts General Laws, requires that a full-time transitional bilingual education program be implemented in every school district where there are 20 LEP students of a single minority language group.

There are 51 such districts (known as the TBE districts) in the state. The language groups include Spanish, "Chinese" (Cantonese, Mandarin, and other dialects), Khmer, Portuguese, Cape Verdean (Kriolu and other dialects), Greek, Italian, Arabic, Armenian, Haitian Creole (several dialects), Laotian, Russian (which includes non-Russian languages of other former Soviet republics), Vietnamese, Hmong, Hebrew, Japanese, Korean, Polish, and Gujarati.

Even if there were enough teachers certified in each of these languages to provide native language instruction, Massachusetts school districts simply could not afford to operate self-contained classrooms with as few as 2 or 3 students (assuming the 20 students in the district are evenly distributed across 13 grades, and two grades are combined in each classroom), as the law stipulates. While programs can be and are split across schools so that grades K and 1 are offered in one school, grades 2 and 3 in another, and so forth, true TBE programs with native language instruction can realistically only be offered in a K-5 school if there are at least 108 students of a single language group (at a pupil/teacher ratio of 18 to 1 as required by the regulations). The numbers required grow substantially at the secondary level when departmentalization occurs (different subjects taught by different teachers). Since teachers then have to be certified in both a subject matter and in a foreign language to teach in a bilingual program, few school districts are able to staff bilingual programs in all subjects at these grade levels. Chapter 2 traces the legislative and political history of bilingual education in the United States and in Massachusetts.

DIFFERENT PROGRAMS FOR DIFFERENT LANGUAGE GROUPS

At the March 30, 1995 hearings on Governor William F. Weld's reform bill, "An Act Relative to Bilingual Education" (HB 1447),

Hispanic[5] students testified in Spanish (subsequently translated by others into English) in favor of transitional bilingual education and against the Governor's bill, which offered school districts the right to state funding for programs that did not include native language instruction. Asian students also testified, but in English, in favor of TBE and against the bill. No one, including the students themselves, acknowledged or even seemed to realize that the programs in which these distinct groups were enrolled bore no resemblance to each other, a fact suggested by the language in which each group testified.

Differences in education programs as a function of the language group are a well-kept secret in Massachusetts and the rest of the United States. According to a study by Young et al. (1984), nationwide at least 40 percent of all LEP children were in programs called TBE, while only 26 percent were in English instruction classrooms in 1982. The other 34 percent were divided among bilingual maintenance, Spanish instruction, and ESL classes. Okada et al. (1983) found *no* projects that reported mastery of English only as a literacy goal for LEP students.[6] The American Legislative Exchange Council (ALEC) and US English (1994) reported 60 percent of the state- and locally funded programs for LEP students were labeled "bilingual education" in 1991-92.[7] Thus, education programs that include native language instruction appear to be the dominant approach to teaching LEP children in the United States.

We use the word "appear" in a deliberate sense, however, since it is clear from visiting classrooms and reading evaluation reports that virtually the only LEP school children receiving native language instruction in the United States according to TBE theory—learning to read and write in the native language and learning subject matter in the native language—are Spanish-speaking elementary students, and even this group does not always receive native language instruction. The instructional environment for Spanish speakers enrolled in programs called TBE can run the gamut from self-contained classrooms with extensive native language instruction to regular classroom enrollment with periodic ESL pullout instruction. Whether any particular Spanish-speaking student receives native language instruction depends on the size of the Spanish-speaking population in the school district and the availability of Spanish-speaking teachers. Based on our observations, no other language minority students, even those enrolled in programs called TBE, actually receive much, if any, native language instruction—regardless of the size of the language group and regardless of the availability of teachers fluent in the language.

Education programs for non-Spanish-speaking LEP students are almost always closer to what we would call structured immersion, even though for political, legal, or funding reasons they may be called TBE. Chapter 4 discusses how the Transitional Bilingual Education Act is actually being implemented in Massachusetts and which students are enrolled in TBE programs. The chapter includes extensive classroom observations; insights gleaned from teachers, administrators, and state officials; and an analysis of results from a survey conducted by the Executive Office of Education of the Commonwealth of Massachusetts.

THE EFFECTIVENESS OF BILINGUAL EDUCATION

"Bilingual education" is thus different things to different people—in practice, there is no single approach called "bilingual education" or even a single approach called "transitional bilingual education." This phenomenon, of course, only complicates the issue of evaluating and analyzing the effects of these programs—as does the difference between elementary and secondary school programs.

Unfortunately, there has been no scientific research conducted in Massachusetts evaluating the TBE programs that have been in place over the last 25 years. Christine Rossell wrote to the 51 TBE districts (those districts with more than 20 LEP students of a single language group) in 1993, asking for recent program evaluations that related program characteristics to educational outcomes. The typical response was that the only evaluations conducted were data requests from the state department of education. Others simply failed to respond. Although there are a few Massachusetts program evaluations in the national Educational Research Information Clearinghouse (ERIC) database in earlier years, none is a scientific evaluation relating program characteristics to educational outcomes. In its 1994 report, the Massachusetts Bilingual Education Commission concludes,

> ...Despite TBE being in place in Massachusetts for 23 years, we don't know whether TBE is effective. In short, we do not know, on the basis of measured outcomes, whether TBE programs in Massachusetts produce good results or poor results. There are no comprehensive data that evaluate the performance of TBE pupils compared with pupils from other groups.[8]

There has been some scientific research conducted in other states and countries over this period. Rossell and Baker (1996) reviewed hundreds of studies conducted from the 1960s to the present.[9] Of the 300 program evaluations we were able to locate, only 72 conformed to the standards for a scientific study. These 72 studies offer no consistent research support for transitional bilingual education as a superior instructional practice for improving the English language achievement of LEP children. Chapter 3 offers a summary of these findings and the second language learning theories espoused by proponents and opponents of bilingual education.

Selecting and Exiting Students in TBE

There are a number of problems with the procedures used to identify children eligible for TBE and to measure their progress.

Home language surveys ask about what language is spoken at home, not the student's own abilities in English. Oral proficiency tests overidentify the number who are actually limited English proficient because the tests cannot tell the difference between a student who is simply limited in English and a student who has other educational problems. Roughly half of English monolingual students who take English oral proficiency tests "fail" them even though English is the only language they know. There are similar problems with standardized achievement tests since they are deliberately constructed so that half the students score below the 50th percentile, 35 percent score below the 35th percentile, and so forth. In sum, fallible instruments overidentify students as LEP; these same instruments prevent some students once in the program from ever getting out.

Thus, the statistics found in federal, state, and local documents on the number of LEP children have a wide margin of error in favor of overidentifying students as LEP. These statistics are not consistent from state to state, school district to school district, nor year to year within school districts and states. Chapter 5 reviews the practices of the state in classifying students as LEP and entering them in and exiting them from TBE programs. This chapter also reviews research and writing on the validity of the practices used in Massachusetts and the rest of the United States.

THE COST OF TRANSITIONAL BILINGUAL EDUCATION

The calculation of the cost of TBE is a complex and lengthy process, which should involve classroom observation and extensive interviews to determine exactly what type of support each student is receiving. While valid cost data are limited, the evidence suggests that TBE is more expensive than the regular classroom and more expensive than other self-contained classroom programs, such as structured immersion, that teach in English, primarily because TBE requires two sets of materials and—by law—a smaller class size. But regular classroom instruction with ESL pullout, a common alternative in Massachusetts and elsewhere, can be more expensive than TBE (depending on its class size) because the former requires paying two teachers. In short, a self-contained classroom with one teacher, regardless of the language of instruction, may be less expensive than a program with one classroom teacher and a pullout program with another teacher; exactly how much less will often depend on the class size for each alternative. Chapter 6 discusses what is known about the cost of bilingual education in Massachusetts and explains how an analysis to determine its true cost should be conducted.

Opinion Surveys on Bilingual Education

Opinion surveys show that the general public, and language minority parents in particular, support special help for LEP children, but many respondents are somewhat confused about what bilingual education means. This is not surprising since many educators and policymakers are similarly confused. Part of the confusion arises from the continued use of "bilingual education" to refer to programs in which students actually learn to read and write in English and learn content area in English, not in their native language.

When language minority parents have been asked to rank the three most important things they wanted their children to learn at school, they have displayed the same attitudes as all American parents—they stressed academics, English language, and then general education. Teaching the non-English language was mentioned by only a very small group, and almost no one mentioned instruction in ethnic heritage. Many language minority parents surveyed wanted their children to become literate in the native language, but they were not willing to give up any part of the regular school day in return.

Chapter 7 summarizes a number of opinion polls on bilingual education and other pedagogical issues. These data come from surveys conducted nationally and in other states and cities. But they are suggestive of what we might find in Massachusetts if we were to conduct a parent or citizen survey.

RECOMMENDATIONS

In light of the many questions surrounding TBE in Massachusetts, we recommend the following legislative and regulatory reforms to improve educational programs for LEP students:

1. *Free School Districts from the Legal Obligation to Provide Native Language Instruction.* The first and most important policy recommendation is that school districts should be freed from the legal obligation to provide programs in native language instruction to LEP children.

   Increase the LEP Population Size Needed to Trigger a Self-Contained Classroom. The law should be changed so that districts are not required to offer a self-contained classroom, regardless of the language of instruction, until the number of LEP students in any given *school* is at least 18 in any particular *grade*. These students do not need to be of the same language group since they can be taught in an all-English, structured immersion program. Nor should students be bused forcibly out of their neighborhood school or otherwise denied their school of choice in order to fill a LEP classroom. In any case, the district should not be obligated to keep a student in such a separate environment for more than one school year.

1. *Require Parental Consent for Enrollment in a Self-Contained Classroom.* Chapter 71A, as currently written, first places the child identified as LEP in transitional bilingual education and then allows parents to withdraw the child by

written notice to the school authorities, thus putting the burden on parents to disagree with the authorities and to disrupt their child's education. We think the burden should be on the school district. Parents should have to give their written consent *before* their child is enrolled in *any* program with a self-contained classroom of LEP students, regardless of the language of instruction.

2. *Require English Language Fluency for Teachers in an Educational Program for LEP Children.* Teachers in educational programs for LEP children should not be granted certificates to teach LEP children unless they possess a bachelor's degree or better from an accredited university in the United States and meet the requirements set by the state board of education for certification in second language acquisition techniques. If the teacher is not a graduate of an academic institution in the United States, he or she should be required to demonstrate fluency in written and spoken English by means of an examination, both oral and written.

3. *Change the Criteria for Entering and Exiting a Self-Contained Classroom.* A home language survey should identify students who are possibly limited English proficient by asking what language is most often spoken by the student. If it is a language other than English, this student should be referred to the Language Appraisal Team for each school or school district. This team should consist of administrators, regular classroom teachers, and teachers of limited-English-proficient children in self-contained classrooms (if they exist in the school). The Language Appraisal Team should also make the decision as to whether a child is ready to be mainstreamed. The classroom teacher's evaluation should be the major factor, not test scores, since teachers are better judges of the ability of students to survive in a regular English language classroom and better able to determine whether students need extra help than are tests of any kind. Except in unusual circumstances, a child should not be in a self-contained classroom for more than a year.

4. *Keep Class Sizes Small.* The class size for self-contained classrooms of LEP students, regardless of the language of instruction, probably should be smaller than that for regular classrooms. Nevertheless, the current limit of 18 students per class (assuming one teacher, without an aide) is arbitrary and not grounded in research.

5. *Better Research.* The Commonwealth of Massachusetts should require local school districts to keep the kind of data that would allow social scientists to analyze variations in programs and the effects of these variations on English language acquisition and academic performance. More quality research needs to be done.

6. *The Ideal Program.* What scientific evidence there is on the effectiveness of alternative instructional programs for LEP children suggests that the best, and most cost-effective, program for LEP children is structured immersion. The language of instruction in a structured immersion program is English at a level the child can understand in a self-contained classroom of LEP students who are at approximately the same level of English language knowledge and the same age. The children in a structured immersion classroom do not have to be of the same language background, but the teacher should be trained in second language acquisition techniques. These programs should be fully integrated into regular schools so that students are exposed to English speakers on the playground, in the cafeterias, the halls, assemblies, and other areas before, during, and after school. LEP students should probably not remain in self-contained classrooms for more than a year, even if the language of instruction is English. Another way of dealing with LEP students with different levels of English is to offer an extended school day for those who are behind.

Chapter 8 gives the authors' conclusions and a thorough presentation of these recommendations.

CHAPTER TWO

THE LEGISLATIVE AND POLITICAL HISTORY OF BILINGUAL EDUCATION

The use of foreign languages in schools in the United States in the 19th and early 20th centuries was largely limited to parochial and private schools. Poles and Italians, for example, established native language instruction in parochial schools in many cities. Other groups established after-school and weekend classes for children to teach their respective languages and cultures. But all of these programs were voluntary and privately funded.

The one exception to this pattern was certain German immigrants, who because of their geographical concentrations were able at various times to establish public school instruction in the native language in some cities in the Midwest and Northeast. German-speaking Americans were operating schools in Philadelphia in their native language as early as 1694, and across the state of Pennsylvania German was a language of instruction in public schools for a brief period in the 1830s.[1] By the mid-1880s, German-English schools were operating in such cities as Baltimore, Cincinnati, Cleveland, Indianapolis, Milwaukee, and St. Louis.[2] Indeed, a school superintendent in 19th-century Marathon County, Wisconsin, argued the need for German programs in the public schools along lines that are often used today:

> The children should first learn to express their thoughts in their mother tongue; they should first learn to read that and afterward they would learn more of the English language in three months than they would learn, in the old way, in three years...Let the child's mind have a chance to enlarge by the use of its own language and it will in time learn another language two times faster and understandingly.[3]

By the end of World War I, however, public school instruc-tion in German or any other non-English language was pretty much a dead issue.

THE CIVIL RIGHTS MOVEMENT YEARS

The civil rights movement of the 1960s revived the issue of native tongue instruction. U.S. Senator Ralph Yarborough (D-Texas) catalyzed Hispanic support for federal intervention on behalf of linguistic minority students by painting a picture of Hispanics as disadvantaged minorities who had been the victims of discrimination. In 1971 national data showed a 37-point gap in com rates between whites and Hispanics favoring whites and a 9-point gap between blacks and Hispanics favoring blacks.[4] Although 1971 was the first year national data on Hispanics were kept separately, there is testimonial evidence of similar white-Hispanic gaps in the 1960s.

Data such as these influenced Congress to pass three statutes to promote greater public school responsiveness to linguistic minority students' needs: 1) the Bilingual Education Act of 1968, also known as Title VII of the Elementary and Secondary Education Act (ESEA); 2) Title VI of the Civil Rights Act of 1964; and 3) the Equal Educational Opportunities Act (EEOA) of 1970. Administrative agencies, such as the Office for Civil Rights (OCR) and the Office of Bilingual Education and Minority Language Affairs (OBEMLA),[5] were created as a result of this legislation and directed to implement these provisions.[6] The federal courts also reviewed several lawsuits during this period, brought by linguistic minorities claiming that school districts had violated the above federal laws by ignoring the language barrier.[7]

The Bilingual Education Act was the first piece of federal legislation devoted exclusively to addressing the needs of linguistic minority students. Although the federal government had dealt earlier with the problems of children disadvantaged by segregation and poverty in the 1964 Civil Rights Act and the 1965 Elementary and Secondary Education Act, bilingual education became an organizing principle for politically active Hispanics who considered themselves uniquely excluded from the educational process by language and cultural problems not addressed in other programs. Bilingual education advocates argued that the reason for Hispanic children on average having lower achievement than white children was the then-current practice of placing Spanish-speaking children in all-English regular classrooms and "forcing" them to give up their native tongue.

Hispanic advocates had high hopes for the 1968 Bilingual Education Act as evidenced by the debate on the subject, but in the end it was nothing more than a modest grant-in-aid program designed to promote research and experimentation. The act provided federal financial assistance to local education agencies (LEAs) to develop and carry out new and different elementary and secondary school programs designed to meet the special educational needs of non-English-speaking and limited-English-speaking students who were poor. Native tongue instruction was not required, however, and the legislation specifically left the type of program to the discretion of local school districts.

The Supreme Court became involved with *Lau v. Nichols* (414 U.S. 563, 1974). The Court, reversing two lower courts on the basis of Title VI of the Civil Rights Act of 1964, held that any school district accepting federal aid must affirmatively overcome the English language deficiencies of students with limited English-speaking ability. The Court was careful, however, to emphasize that *no specific remedy* was required under the statute. This opinion is particularly important because it had the effect of validating OCR's 1970 memorandum interpreting Title VI of the 1964 Civil Rights Act as encompassing the denial of equal educational opportunity to language minority children. It validated as well OCR's request that school districts file compliance plans.

The *Lau* decision also motivated OCR to assemble an education task force to recommend policy alternatives for compliance with the *Lau* decision. The OCR task force recommendations, known as the "Lau remedies," went well beyond the Court's requirement that school districts do something for LEP children. The task force insisted that transitional bilingual education was the best, if not the only, instructional approach for providing equal educational opportunity to linguistic minorities. Without ever holding a public discussion of this decision, OCR negotiated education plans with more than 500 individual school districts between 1975 and 1980. School districts that did not wish to provide TBE had to prove that their alternative programs were as effective, even though OCR itself had never proven that TBE was effective.

By 1974, the Bilingual Education Act of 1968 (Title VII) had been amended—the poverty criterion was dropped, and native tongue instruction was added "to the extent necessary to allow a child to progress effectively through the educational system."

The 1978 amendments also included the use of the native language "to the extent necessary to allow a child to achieve competence in the English language." At the same time student eligibility for assistance was expanded to all children of "limited English proficiency" so long as they still needed help with reading and writing skills. Finally, the amendments addressed the problem of language minority segregation by allowing the enrollment of up to 40 percent English-proficient children in bilingual programs.

On August 5, 1980, just three months before the presidential election, the Carter administration proposed Lau regulations that were even more prescriptive than the Lau remedies because they mandated for the first time bilingual education in schools where at least 25 LEP children of the same minority language group were enrolled in two consecutive elementary grades (K through 8). Controversy over the proposed regulations prompted Congress to block the rules from taking effect until after the election.

The Reagan Years

Ronald Reagan's 1980 landslide victory and a US Department of Education review of the research literature, conducted by Keith Baker and Adriana de Kanter (1981), motivated OCR to retreat on the proposed new rules.[8] The widely publicized Baker and de Kanter study created a good deal of controversy by concluding that evidence for the effectiveness of bilingual education was tenuous at best and therefore the federal government had no basis for requiring it. As a result, the Reagan administration withdrew the proposed Lau regulations in 1981. OCR's efforts to ensure compliance with Title VII fell off sharply after that as school districts were no longer required to abide by the Lau remedies.

The 1984 Bilingual Education Act provided more flexibility for state and local school districts. The act allowed up to 4 percent of overall funds (or up to 10 percent if more than $140 million was appropriated in a single fiscal year) to go to alternative instructional programs for LEP students that did not use the native tongue.

The 1988 reauthorization included further provisions to allow school districts to use different approaches to the education of LEP children. Part A authorized 75 percent of total grant funds to school districts for transitional bilingual education, but increased to 25 percent the amount of grant funds that could go to alternative instructional programs that did *not* use the native tongue. In addition, a three-year limit was placed on a student's participation in a transitional bilingual education program or in alternative instructional programs, although under special circumstances a student could continue in a program for up to two additional years.

THE 1994 REAUTHORIZATION

In 1994, the Elementary and Secondary Education Act was reauthorized as the "Improving America's Schools Act," although Title VII of that act is still called "The Bilingual Education Act." This reauthorization, appropriating $215 million for fiscal year 1995, gave funding priority to programs that provide for the development of proficiency both in English and another language and kept the 25 percent maximum allocation for programs that did not use the native tongue. What is different from the reauthorizations under the Republican administrations, however, is that the alternative educational programs must be justified by 1) small numbers of language minority students (although no minimum is mentioned) or 2) a lack of teachers with native language skills (after demonstrating an effort to obtain such).

THE HISTORY OF BILINGUAL EDUCATION IN MASSACHUSETTS

The first state to enact its own legislation was Massachusetts, which in 1971 passed Chapter 71A, the Transitional Bilingual Education Act, requiring native tongue instruction for children who were limited- or non-English speakers.[9] Today 30 states permit native tongue instruction, but Massachusetts is one of only nine states that require it.

As figure 2-1 indicates,[10] in 1970 (the three bars on the left side of the graph) Massachusetts Hispanics had a high school completion rate 11 percentage points lower than whites (although seven points higher than blacks). Armed with data such as these, as well as OCR recommendations, Massachusetts Hispanic leaders lobbied for state legislation requiring native tongue instruction. The argument made in Massachusetts was pretty much the same being made nationally: if Hispanic children were dropping out of school at higher rates and achieving at lower rates than white children, the problem must have been the then-current practice of instructing LEP children in English—an alien language.

Figure 2–1
% of Each Group (25 Years and Older)
Completing High School in Massachusetts
1970 and 1989

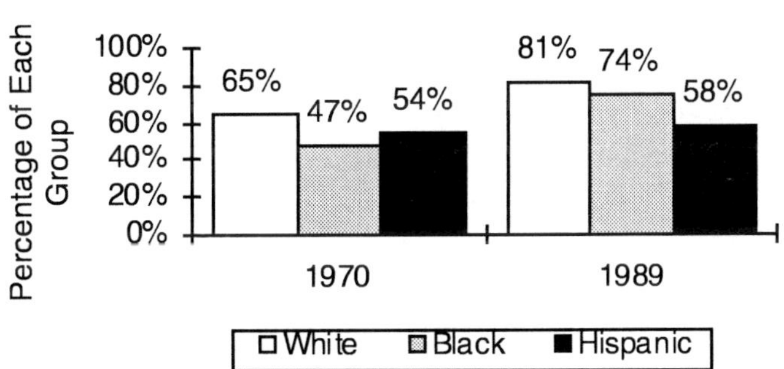

Source: U.S. Bureau of the Census, *Statistical Abstract of the United States*, Washington, D.C.: Government Printing Office, 1991, tables 224 & 227.

Note: These statistics must be interpreted with caution, as this group (25 years and older) includes people who, because of historical patterns, are less likely to have completed high school.

According to Hailer (1976), who was Assistant Secretary in the Executive Office of Educational Affairs during this time period, the authors of the Massachusetts law were Robert Crabtree, research director for the Massachusetts Legislature's Joint Committee on Education from 1968 to 1973, and a team of lawyers from Harvard, including Stuart Abelson and Jeffrey Kobrick.[11] Ernest Mazzone was the state department of education's legislative liaison in drafting the legislation, which was cosponsored by the Massachusetts Teachers Association.

One of the key figures in drafting and lobbying for the bill was Sister Francis Georgia Vicente, a Catholic nun from Boston who had been working with the Boston Spanish-speaking community through the Mayor's Office of Public Service. She subsequently was appointed Advocate for Linguistic Minorities in the Bureau of Equal Educational Opportunity. The outcome of all this political action—a requirement for native tongue instruction—is attributed by Hailer (1976) to the influence of Vicente and the 37-member Massachusetts Advisory Council on Bilingual Education chaired by Alex Rodriguez.[12] In 1972, Ernest Mazzone became the first director of the Bureau of Transitional Bilingual Education, created by Chapter 71A.

CHAPTER 71A

The law itself, Chapter 71A (reproduced in appendix 2-1), is only five single-spaced pages; the regulations and guidelines take up another 90 pages. Section I of Chapter 71A defines the terms used. Of particular importance is the definition of "children of limited English-speaking ability"[13] as those of foreign birth or from a home with non-English-speaking parents, who also cannot perform "ordinary classwork in English."

It is relatively easy to determine foreign birth or a non-English-speaking home environment by means of the home language survey—

a card included in public school registration materials asking for information on the child's first language and languages spoken at home. The hard part is accurately and consistently determining who is "incapable of performing ordinary classwork in English." None of the oral English proficiency tests currently used to identify LEP students can distinguish between a student who has a language barrier and a student who has other educational problems (see chapter 5).

The other important definition in Chapter 71A is that of a "program in transitional bilingual education." This definition *requires* that

- the program be full-time
- all courses and subjects be given in the native language as well as English
- the child be taught to read and write in the native language and in English
- the child be taught the history and culture of the native country and the United States.

Section 2 of 71A further requires that this program be provided in every school district with 20 or more LEP children of a single language. This means that a school district with only 20 LEP students of one language group could be forced to maintain extremely small self-contained classes (even if all the students were bused to the same school and two grades were combined in each classroom). No school district in Massachusetts could afford this.[14] While the regulations do allow up to four grades to be combined, few educators feel this is pedagogically defensible.

Section 2 also provides that LEP children must be enrolled in a TBE program for a period of three years or until they demonstrate sufficient English proficiency "to perform successfully" in classes in which instruction is given only in English. School districts can, however, keep a LEP child in a TBE program longer than three years subject to the approval of the school committee and the parents, and no child can be transferred out earlier than three years unless the parents approve and the child has achieved a certain score on the exit test. If the child does not perform adequately in the regular classroom upon exiting TBE, he or she can be put back into the program. Many children stay in a TBE program throughout their elementary school careers, which raises the question of how valid the procedures are that are used to determine whether a child is "performing successfully" in an all-English classroom (see chapter 5).[15]

Section 6 of 71A deals with the certification of TBE teachers. They are not required to meet the general certification requirements in section 38G of Chapter 71. While teachers must demonstrate speaking and reading ability in the non-English language they will be teaching in, they must have only communicative skills in English. Thus, the law allows for the possibility that students in self-contained TBE classrooms may be receiving English instruction from a teacher who is not qualified to teach it, since in TBE programs it is the TBE teacher who provides English language instruction, not a different ESL teacher. If there is a shortage of qualified TBE teachers, a teacher may be allowed to teach who does not meet TBE certification requirements. Since the standard for English skills is so low, however, teachers on waivers are most likely to be limited in the native tongue, not in English.

THE REGULATIONS

The regulations relevant to Chapter 71A are described most fully and recently in a 1992 Massachusetts Department of Education publication titled *Educating Language Minority Students*. The most important components of the regulations have to do with reimbursement. According to the 1992 publication, the state department of education at one time paid only the cost of educating a student in TBE above the average per-pupil expenditure for regular students, and it was estimated that a reasonable reimbursement would be $250 to $500 per pupil enrolled in TBE.[16] Regulations adopted in 1978 created a formula for state reimbursement based on hours in the program and days of participation.

These regulations have since been superseded by the so-called "foundation" funding formula, which is part of the 1993 Education Reform Act. The new system focuses state education resources on poorer districts that spend less on public education than an amount specified in their respective foundation budgets, which are determined by multiplying "foundation enrollment" by a standard expense model (including localized wage adjustments). These budgets are based in part on a staffing model that assumes one teacher for every 15 LEP students. The budgets are also constructed by counting each LEP student twice in the foundation enrollment.

The regulations require that the maximum student-teacher ratio be 18 to 1, or 25 to 1 if a native-language-speaking teacher's aide is assigned to the class. In multi-grade classrooms, the ratio is 15 to 1 or 20 to 1 with an aide, but the age spread in a classroom cannot be more than 4 years, except in kindergarten where it cannot be more than one year. School districts with programs enrolling 200 or more children must appoint a TBE director, supervisor, or supervising teacher.[17]

Program Evaluation

Each school district must appoint a committee of three or more members, including at least one representative from the school administration, the TBE program, and the Parent Advisory Committee (PAC), to conduct an annual review of its TBE program. The PAC must have at least five members including at least one representative from each language group for which a TBE program is offered. No guidelines are given as to what this review should encompass or how it should take place. It is likely it would be no more than an input-based evaluation, since across the United States virtually all the evaluations required by law are of this type. An input-based evaluation simply attempts to determine if the regulated entity (in this case a school district) is conforming to the law and if the clients (parents and children) are relatively happy with the services they are receiving. This kind of an evaluation is not considered a scientific test of the effectiveness of a program.

Program Models

In 1989, Chapter 71A was amended, and in May 1990 the Bureau of Transitional Bilingual Education became the Bureau of Equity and Language Services. (This bureau disappeared in May 1993 when the state department of education moved from Quincy to Malden and reorganized into service clusters based on functions.) In 1991 guidelines and program models were developed, expanding the types of bilingual education programs from one (i.e., TBE) to six:

- Transitional Bilingual Education
- Two-Way Bilingual Programs
- Accelerated Basic Skills Program
- Advanced Basic Skills Program High School
- Integrative Bilingual Education Program
- Maintenance Program.

The guidelines acknowledge that Massachusetts law goes beyond federal law in requiring that "transitional programs in bilingual education must have a native language literacy component, i.e. that the reading and writing of the native language must be taught."[18]

The five additional models (beyond the core model—TBE) all require some native tongue instruction, but the Two-Way program includes monolingual English speakers, so the "native tongue" instruction includes English. The Accelerated Basic Skills program is for students who are in grades three through eight and are three to five years behind their age peers academically. The Advanced Basic Skills program is for students who are in grades 9 through 12 and are three to five years behind their age peers.

The description in the regulations of the Integrative Bilingual Education Program suggests the existence of parallel self-contained bilingual and regular English classrooms with LEP students moving back and forth between them. The actual implemented program (see chapter 4), however, seems to be one of LEP students enrolled in and participating in the regular all-English classroom virtually all day. The TBE teacher is a classroom resource and pulls students out if they need extra help. The TBE teacher may also assign special lessons for new students or those who want to maintain their native language skills.

The final program type is the Bilingual Program Maintenance, which does not have as its goal the transitioning of students into a regular English classroom. Its goal is to produce fully bilingual students. Thus, a student could theoretically stay in this kind of bilingual program his or her entire academic career.

THE META CONSENT DECREE OF 1992

On November 30, 1992, a plaintiff group representing the Lynn Hispanic Parents Advisory Committee, the Chelsea Hispanic Parents Advisory Council, and the Parents United for the Education and Development of Others, whose legal counsel is META (Multicultural Education, Training and Advocacy, Inc.), entered into an agreement with the Massachusetts Board of Education and Department of Education after having filed a suit, *Lynn Hispanic Parents Advisory Committee, et al. v. Commissioner of the Massachusetts Department of Education, et al.* (CA 85-2475-H). The suit alleged improper monitoring on the part of the state. The state agreed, without admitting liability, to conduct annual on-site reviews of each school district with more than 200 students enrolled in a TBE program[19] and on-site reviews every three years of TBE programs in districts with 200 or fewer students. If a school district with more than 200 students is found to be in compliance in one year, it is exempt for the next two years.

In addition, school districts with increasing enrollment in one or more language groups will come under surveillance when the number reaches between 15 and 19 in the third year. Any such districts are required to document their procedures for identification of LEP students, determination of their proficiency, and determination of appropriate instructional placement. If the LEP students are not receiving "language services in accordance with ...[Chapter] 71A,...and [Chapter] 76, and the regulations thereunder, the Department shall take such further action as it deems appropriate..." (p. 6). Implicit in this requirement is the assumption that districts with enrollment increasing to just below 20 will try to cheat on their classification procedures and/or educational practices in order to avoid reaching the "triggering point." In other words, META (and the state) continue to act as if the number 20 is a meaningful number and that surpassing it actually does produce a real TBE program.

THE EDUCATION REFORM ACT OF 1993

The final development in the history of bilingual education in Massachusetts is the Education Reform Act of 1993. While not specifically aimed at TBE, there are several provisions in the 111-page document that affect it. First, the Education Reform Act establishes a

12-member, unpaid advisory council to the Board of Education on bilingual education. Six of the members of this board are to be parents of "bilingual students" [sic]. This probably means that six members must be the parents of students enrolled in a TBE program.

The law also provides for "competency determination" as a condition of high school graduation (p. 19). One of the areas of competency is English, and there is no mention in the law that TBE or LEP students will be excluded from this requirement. Since this part of the law has yet to be implemented, no compromise or determination of how LEP students are to be affected has been made.

One aspect of the law that is specifically aimed at LEP students is found on p. 25:

> All potential English proficient students from language groups in which programs of transitional bilingual education are offered under chapter seventy-one A shall also be allowed opportunities for assessment of their performance in the language which best allows them to demonstrate educational achievement and mastery. For the purposes of this section, a "potential English proficient student" shall be defined as a student who is not able to perform ordinary class work in English; provided, however, that no student shall be allowed to be tested in a language other than English for longer than three consecutive years.

Nowhere in the document does it explain *why* such a student should be tested in his or her native language or how one is to interpret the score. Nor is there any recognition of the problems of equivalency of tests given in different languages and the problems of internal validity or the reliability of tests given in languages other than English.

The Education Reform Act also requires that each school district not only provide a TBE program as described in Chapter 71A but provide extensive information to the state department of education, including information on the "academic progress" of students who have completed a program in transitional bilingual education. Once again, there is no discussion of how information on academic progress is to be presented nor is there even a definition of the term. Is it to be simple descriptive data of the type that appears regularly in the newspapers, such as the average scores of students or the rate of increase in their scores over a year? Is it grades or high school graduation rates? If simple descriptive data is all that is required of school districts, it will tell the department very little about the academic progress of students and the effectiveness of a school district's programs.

Because the nature of instruction in a TBE program is strongly affected by variations in the language skills of teachers, written materials in a language, the size of the language minority population, and parental support for native tongue instruction, a valid assessment must include considerable observation of the classroom to determine exactly how the program is implemented. Valid assessment is further complicated by the students' diverse home environments. Sophisticated statistical techniques must be used to differentiate the effect of any educational program from the effect of the home environment where students spend most of their time (and which currently explains roughly 80 to 90 percent of the variation in academic achievement).[20] The cost and time involved in conducting this kind of sophisticated statistical modeling is simply ignored in the Education Reform Act, which is rife with vague prescriptions, such as the following:

> Schools that have consistently failed to improve the academic performance of their students shall be deemed underperforming, in accordance with the board's regulations (p. 28).

What does this mean? It is a common assumption that the Boston Public Schools are doing a poor job of educating students. However, the data presented to support this conclusion are typically comparative, showing only that Boston Public School students have lower scores than those of the surrounding suburbs. No attempt is ever made to control for the home environment differences between school districts. It is quite possible that the Wellesley, Newton, Brookline, and Concord schools produce smaller achievement gains in their students, after eliminating the effect of home environment, than do the Boston Public Schools. Because no one does the correct analysis, we do not know.

The Education Reform Act also requires school districts with language minority students to "address the need for training and skills in second language acquisition and in working with culturally and linguistically diverse student populations" in their professional development plan for teaching staff. There is no explanation of what "address" means.

Finally, the act appointed a "special commission to study the effectiveness and implementation of bilingual education programs in the commonwealth." After more than a year of work, the commission produced *Striving for Success: The Education of Bilingual Pupils.*[21] While it contains a number of sensible recommendations, it adds little to what is currently known by academics and local school administrators because a) it is a consensus document written by a committee comprised of individuals with diverse views, and b) there is little valid data by which to evaluate bilingual education practices and procedures.

The issue of bilingual education has continued to be controversial, and each spring for much of the last decade a reform bill has been introduced that would provide for more flexibility in offering help to LEP children. Reform is still on the legislative agenda because the educational attainment gap between whites and Hispanics used to justify native tongue instruction in 1971 still exists decades after bilingual education was implemented throughout the state. Unlike the United States as a whole, Massachusetts (one of the few states requiring native tongue instruction in TBE) experienced from 1970 to 1989 a widening gap between high school completion rates for whites and Hispanics. Figure 2-1 shows that in 1989 (the three bars on the right), 18 years after Chapter 71A, the high school completion rate for whites was 23 percentage points higher than the rate for Hispanics. In addition, while in 1970 blacks in Massachusetts had a high school completion rate 7 percentage points lower than Massachusetts Hispanics, in 1989 the rate for blacks was 16 percentage points higher than for Hispanics.

Not only are high school completion rates for Hispanics still much lower than for whites, so is academic achievement. Figure 2-2 shows the percentage of Asians, whites, Hispanics, and blacks scoring at or above the proficient level in mathematics on a national test given in 1992 by the National Center for Education Statistics.[22] Thirty percent of Asian and 28 percent of white 4th graders scored at or above the proficient level in mathematics; only 9 percent of Hispanics and 2 percent of blacks did so.[23] Similar results are found at the 8th grade level: 31 percent of whites, but only 8 percent of Hispanics and 5 percent of black students, achieved at or above the proficient level.

These statistics, however, are merely descriptive, not causal. We cannot know the effect of educational programs on educational attainment until we control for differences between the groups. But it is exactly these kinds of data that were used to justify Chapter 71A in the first place and that keep it embroiled in controversy.

Figure 2–2
% of Each Group At or Above Proficient Level in Mathematics in 4th and 8th Grade in Massachusetts, 1992

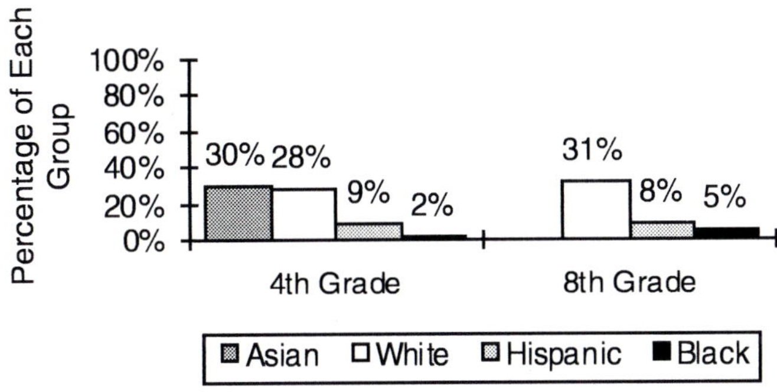

Source: National Center for Education Statistics, NAEP 1992 *Mathematics Report Card for the Nation and the States*, Washington, D.C.: Government Printing Office, 1992: 99, 101.
Note: No data for Asian 8th graders due to insufficient sample size.

The achievement gap is of increasing relevance for Massachusetts because the proportion of the state's public school population identified as language minority is increasing, and it is these students who receive TBE. The white population has declined from 88 percent in 1982 to 79 percent in 1994. The largest relative increase has been among Hispanics—from 4 percent of the student population in 1982 to 9 percent in 1994. Asians have similarly increased from 2 percent of the population in 1982 to 4 percent in 1994.[24]

CONCLUSION

Chapter 71A ignores the fiscal realities that Massachusetts school districts face, making full compliance difficult if not impossible for many districts. The general consensus among Massachusetts Department of Education officials and local school district administrators is that the number 20 as a triggering device for TBE is unrealistic. Indeed, no one seems to know where the number came from, and many agree it would make more sense for the requirement to be 20 per grade as it is in many other states. Even then students would often have to be bused to a single school.

The monitoring process required by Chapter 71A and the 1992 Consent Decree is a further burden on the state and on school districts. In addition, the likelihood that it will produce meaningful results is low. It is impossible for this kind of monitoring system to work properly given how much training would be necessary and how much controversy, both political and pedagogical, there is over how LEP students should be taught.

Appendix 2-1

Chapter 71A
TRANSITIONAL BILINGUAL EDUCATION

71A:1. DEFINITIONS

Section 1. The following words, as used in this chapter shall, unless the context requires otherwise, have the following meanings:

"Department", the department of education.

"School committee", the school committee of a city, town or regional school district.

"Children of limited English-speaking ability", (1) children who were not born in the United States whose native tongue is a language other than English and who are incapable of performing ordinary classwork in English; and (2) children who were born in the United States of non-English speaking parents and who are incapable of performing ordinary classwork in English.

"Teacher of transitional bilingual education", a teacher with a speaking and reading ability in a language other than English in which bilingual education is offered and with communicative skills in English.

"Program in transitional bilingual education", a full-time program of instruction (1) in all those courses or subjects which a child is required by law to receive and which are required by the child's school committee which shall be given in the native language of the children of limited English-speaking ability who are enrolled in the program and also in English, (2) in the reading and writing of the native language of the children of limited English-speaking ability who are enrolled in the program and in the oral comprehension, speaking, reading and writing of English, and (3) in the history and culture of the country, territory or geographic area which is the native land of the parents of children of limited English-speaking ability who are enrolled in the program and in the history and culture of the United States.

71A:2. LANGUAGE CLASSIFICATION OF CHILDREN; ESTABLISHMENT OF PROGRAM; PERIOD OF PARTICIPATION; EXAMINATION

Section 2. Each school committee shall ascertain, not later than the first day of March, under regulations prescribed by the department, the number of children of limited English-speaking ability within their school system, and shall classify them according to the language of which they possess a primary speaking ability.

When, at the beginning of any school year, there are within a city, town or school district not including children who are enrolled in existing private school systems, twenty or more children of limited English-speaking ability in any such language classification, the school committee shall establish, for each classification, a program in transitional bilingual education for the children therein; provided, however, that a school committee may establish a program in transitional bilingual education with respect to any classification with less than twenty children therein.

Every school-age child of limited English-speaking ability not enrolled in existing private school systems shall be enrolled and participate in the program in transitional bilingual education established for the classification to which he belongs by the city, town or school district in which he resides for a period of three years or until such time as he achieves a level of English language skills which will enable him to perform successfully in classes in which instruction is given only in English, whichever shall first occur.

A child of limited English-speaking ability enrolled in a program in transitional bilingual education may, in the discretion of the school committee and subject to the approval of the child's parent or legal guardian, continue in that program for a period longer than three years.

An examination in the oral comprehension, speaking, reading and writing of English, as prescribed by the department, shall be administered annually to all children of limited English-speaking ability enrolled and participating in a program in transitional bilingual education. No school committee shall transfer a child of limited English-speaking ability out of a program in transitional bilingual education prior to his third year of enrollment therein unless the parents of the child approve the transfer in writing, and unless the child has received a score on said examination which, in the determination of the department, reflects a level of English language skills appropriate to his or her grade level.

If later evidence suggests that a child so transferred is still handicapped by an inadequate command of English, he may be reenrolled in the program for a length of time equal to that which remained at the time he was transferred.

71A:3. Notice of Enrollment; Content; Rights of Parents

Section 3. No later than ten days after the enrollment of any child in a program in transitional bilingual education the school committee of the city, town or the school district in which the child resides shall notify by mail the parents or legal guardian of the child of the fact that their child has been enrolled in a program in transitional bilingual education. The notice shall contain a simple, non-technical description of the purposes, method and content of the program in which the child is enrolled and shall inform the parents that they have the right to visit transitional bilingual education classes in which their child is enrolled and to come to the school for a conference to explain the nature of transitional bilingual education. Said notice shall further inform the parents that they have the absolute right, if they so wish, to withdraw their child from a program in transitional bilingual education in the manner as hereinafter provided.

The notice shall be in writing in English and in the language of which the child of the parents so notified possesses a primary speaking ability.

Any parent whose child has been enrolled in a program in transitional bilingual education shall have the absolute right, either at the time of the original notification of enrollment or at the close of any semester thereafter, to withdraw his child from said program by written notice to the school authorities of the school in which his child is enrolled or to the school committee of the city, town or the school district in which his child resides.

71A:4. NON-RESIDENT CHILDREN; ENROLLMENT AND TUITION; JOINT PROGRAMS.

Section 4. A school committee may allow a non-resident child of limited English-speaking ability to enroll in or attend its program in transitional bilingual education and the tuition for such a child shall be paid by the city, town, or the district in which he resides.

Any city, town or school district may join with any other city, town, school district or districts to provide the programs in transitional bilingual education required or permitted by this chapter.

71A:5. PARTICIPATION IN EXTRA-CURRICULAR ACTIVITIES OF PUBLIC SCHOOLS; PLACEMENT OF CHILDREN

Section 5. Instruction in courses of subjects included in a program of transitional bilingual education which are not mandatory may be given in a language other than English. In those courses or subjects in which verbalization is not essential to an understanding of the subject matter, including but not necessarily limited to art, music and physical education, children of limited English-speaking ability shall participate fully with their English-speaking contemporaries in the regular public school classes provided for said subjects. Each school committee of every city, town or school district shall ensure to children enrolled in a program in transitional bilingual education practical and meaningful opportunity to participate fully in the extra-curricular activities of the regular public schools in the city, town or district. Programs in transitional bilingual education shall, whenever feasible, be located in the regular public schools of the city, town or the district rather than separate facilities.

Children enrolled in a program of transitional bilingual education whenever possible shall be placed in classes with children of approximately the same age and level of educational attainment. If children of different age groups or educational levels are combined, the school committee so combining shall ensure that the instruction given each child is appropriate to his or her level of educational attainment and the city, town or the school districts shall keep adequate records of the educational level and progress of each child enrolled in a program. The maximum student-teacher ratio shall be set by the department and shall reflect the special educational needs of children enrolled in programs in transitional bilingual education.

71A:6. Teacher's Certification and Certificate; Qualifications and Requirements; Compensation; Exemptions

Section 6. The board of education, hereinafter called the board, shall grant certificates to teachers of transitional bilingual education who possess such qualifications as are prescribed in this section. The requirements of section thirty-eight G of chapter seventy-one shall not apply to the certification of teachers of transitional bilingual education. Teachers of transitional bilingual education, including those serving under exemptions as provided in this section, shall be compensated by local school committees not less than a step on the regular salary schedule applicable to permanent teachers certified under said section thirty-eight G.

The board shall grant certificates to teachers of transitional bilingual education who present the board with satisfactory evidence that they (1) possess a speaking and reading ability in a language, other than English, in which bilingual education is offered and communicative skills in English; (2) are in good health, provided that no applicant shall be disqualified because of blindness or defective hearing; (3) are of sound moral character; (4) possess a bachelor's degree or an earned higher academic degree or are graduates of a normal school approved by the board; (5) meet such requirements as to courses of study, semester hours therein, experience and training as may be required by the board; and (6) are legally present in the United States and possess legal authorization for employment.

For the purpose of certifying teachers of transitional bilingual education the board may approve programs at colleges or universities devoted to the preparation of such teachers. The institution shall furnish the board with a student's transcript and shall certify to the board that the student has completed the approved program and is recommended for a teaching certificate.

No person shall be eligible for employment by a school committee as a teacher of transitional bilingual education unless he has been granted a certificate by the board; provided, however, that a school committee may prescribe such additional qualifications, approved by the board. Any school committee may upon its request be exempted from the certification requirements of this section for any school year in which compliance therewith would in the opinion of the department constitute a hardship in the securing of teachers of transitional bilingual education in the city, town or regional school district. Exemptions granted under this section shall be subject to annual renewal by the department.

A teacher of transitional bilingual education serving under an exemption as provided in this section shall be granted a certificate if he achieves the requisite qualifications therefor. Two years of service by a teacher of transitional bilingual education under such an exemption shall be credited to the teacher in acquiring the status of serving at the discretion of the school committee as provided in section forty-one of chapter seventy-one, and said two years shall be deemed to immediately precede, and be consecutive with, the year in which a teacher becomes certified. In requesting an exemption under this section a school committee shall give preference to persons who have been certified as teachers in their country or place of national origin.

All holders of certificates and legal exemptions under the provisions of section thirty-eight G of chapter seventy-one who provide the board with satisfactory evidence that they possess a speaking and reading ability in a language other than English may be certified under this section as a teacher of transitional bilingual education.

Nothing in this chapter shall be deemed to prohibit a school committee from employing to teach in a program in transitional bilingual education a teacher certified under section thirty-eight G of chapter seventy-one, so long as such employment is approved by the department.

71A:7. PRE-SCHOOL OR SUMMER SCHOOL PROGRAMS

Section 7. A school committee may establish on a full or part-time basis pre-school or summer school programs in transitional bilingual education for children of limited English-speaking ability or join with the other cities, towns, or school districts in establishing such pre-school or summer programs. Pre-school or summer programs in transitional bilingual education shall not substitute for programs in transitional bilingual education required to be provided during the regular school year.

71A:8. REIMBURSEMENT OF TRANSPORTATION COSTS

Section 8. The state treasurer shall annually, on or before November twentieth, reimburse any city, town, regional school district or independent vocational school for expenditures incurred during the previous fiscal year in the transportation of any pupil enrolled in a transitional bilingual education program and who resides at least one and one-half miles from the school which the pupil attends, as measured by a commonly travelled route, in the manner hereinafter defined. Such reimbursements shall include: first, an amount for each pupil which is equal to the average transportation services expenditure per pupil, enrolled in regular day program in said city, town, regional school district or independent vocational school during said fiscal year, provided that each such pupil enrolled in regular day program resides at least one and one-half miles from the school which said pupil attends; and second, the entire amount by which the average transportation services expenditure per pupil enrolled in such a bilingual program in said city, town, regional school district or independent vocational school during said fiscal year may exceed the aforesaid average transportation services expenditure per pupil enrolled in regular day program. In no instance, however, shall the amount or reimbursement for such excess cost per pupil exceed one hundred and ten percent of the average of such excess costs per pupil in all cities, towns, regional school districts and independent vocational schools in the commonwealth during the fiscal year in which such expenditures were made.

In determining each said average transportation services expenditure per pupil enrolled in regular day program in each city, town, regional school district and independent vocational school, the department of education shall use the transportation services expenditure per pupil eligible for reimbursement under sections seven A, seven B, or sixteen C of chapter seventy-one, whichever is higher, during the same fiscal year. The commissioner of education may, by regulation, under the direction of the state board of education, further define the expenditures per pupil to be used in aforesaid computations.

71A:9. Rules and Regulations; Promulgation

Section 9. In addition to the powers and duties prescribed in previous sections of this chapter, the department shall exercise its authority and promulgate rules and regulations to achieve the full implementation of all provisions of this chapter. A copy of the rules and regulations issued by the department shall be sent to all cities, towns and school districts participating in transitional bilingual education.

CHAPTER THREE

THE EDUCATIONAL EFFECTIVENESS OF BILINGUAL EDUCATION

Despite the widespread acceptance of transitional bilingual education among policymakers, one question continues to be asked by those who read even a little of the research: Are TBE programs effective? Even well-known supporters of bilingual education have questioned its research foundations. Kenji Hakuta concludes, in *Mirror of Language,*

> There is a sober truth that even the ardent advocate of bilingual education would not deny. Evaluation studies of the effectiveness of bilingual education in improving either English or math scores have not been overwhelmingly in favor of bilingual education....An awkward tension blankets the lack of empirical demonstration of the success of bilingual education programs. Someone promised bacon, but it's not there.[1]

Thomas Carter, despite being an advocate of bilingual education and an expert witness for LEP Hispanic plaintiffs in several bilingual education court cases over the last decade, begins a 1986 article with "Regardless of the many roots of the debate, one issue is unresolved. Does bilingual education work?"[2]

Christina Bratt Paulston, a well-known linguist and advocate of bilingual education, makes some telling points in her 1982 report to the National Swedish Board of Education. With regard to transitional bilingual education in the United States, she notes,

> The rationale for bilingual programs is that they are more efficient in teaching English although there is not much hard

> data to support such a view; it has however been the standard argument...The Canadians believe, *with justification,* that fluent proficiency in the target language only occurs when that language is used as a medium of instruction [emphasis added].[3]

She also approvingly cites Toukomaa, another bilingual education advocate, who writes,

> We wish to dissociate ourselves from those arguments, for teaching in the mother tongue, which attempt to frighten parents into choosing mother tongue-teaching by threatening emotional and intellectual under-development in those children who do not receive mother tongue-teaching. Teaching in the mother tongue does not seem to have the magical effect on the child's development, for good or for ill, which it has sometimes been ascribed.[4]

The Association for Supervision and Curriculum Development, an organization of 90,000 principals, school superintendents, teachers, and other educational leaders, noted in a 1987 report on bilingual education, "It is unclear which approach is better [teaching children in English or in their native tongue]."[5]

RESEARCH REVIEWS

There have been a number of extensive reviews of the literature on the effectiveness of TBE for LEP students.[6] None of these reviews, however, has provided a definitive answer to the central question—Does TBE produce greater educational achievement in LEP children than any other education program? Indeed, we sometimes wonder, given the ideological fervor surrounding this issue and the limitations of social science research, whether a definitive answer can ever be provided to the satisfaction of both sides on the debate.

Rossell and Baker (1996) updates our previous reviews of the available research, conducted in the early and mid-1980s.[7] The strategy for Rossell and Baker (1996) was to begin with the studies reviewed in Baker and de Kanter (1983) and Rossell and Ross (1986) and to add to them.[8] The total number of studies and books we have read now numbers above 500, of which 300 are program evaluations, in the sense that their purpose is to evaluate the effectiveness of actual TBE practice or some other second language acquisition technique.

METHODOLOGICAL APPROACH

Each of the 300 program evaluations[9] was assessed to determine if it addressed the relevant questions with a methodologically sound research design. Acceptable studies generally had the following characteristics:

1) They were true experiments in which students were randomly assigned to "treatment" and control groups. Random assignment eliminates the bias that occurs when students are self-selected—when parents are permitted to volunteer their children for a program. It also eliminates the bias that occurs when a school district selects students for a program on the basis of achievement. If program participants were self-selected or selected by the district, the evaluator cannot be sure whether the outcomes observed are reflective of the program itself or biased by the selection process.

2) If they had non-random assignment, they either matched students in the treatment and comparison groups on factors that influence achievement or statistically controlled for them. Among the important factors affecting the performance of language minority children in school, especially in learning English, are the following: age, socioeconomic status, ethnicity, student motivation and self-concept, parental support for the educational program, the language and environment of the community, cognitive ability, place of birth—immigrant or native-born—and degree of home-language dominance.[10] If the composition of one program is substantially different from that

of another program on any of these dimensions, one cannot know if the outcomes are a result of the program or of these other factors unless one statistically controls for these other factors.

3) Outcome measures were in English using NCEs (normal curve equivalents), raw scores, scale scores, percentiles, etc., but not grade equivalents.

4) Additional educational interventions were non-existent, or the study controlled for them.

5) Appropriate statistical tests were applied. There are statistical tests that are designed to take into account the number of subjects in each group, the size of the outcome difference between the groups, and the variation in outcomes within groups that must be performed in order to verify that the results are "statistically significant"—that they could not have happened by chance.

Analysis of covariance was by far the most common statistical method used to control for pre-existing differences in non-experimental studies.[11] Many statisticians have serious reservations about whether this method succeeds in properly adjusting pre-existing differences. Similarly there are doubts that matching students on important characteristics that influence achievement is entirely successful. Nevertheless, we generally accepted both methods unless there were serious defects in their application.

FINDINGS

Seventy-two of the studies and program evaluations reviewed were deemed methodologically acceptable. These studies seek to demonstrate the effect of transitional bilingual education on second language (usually English) reading, language, and/or mathematics compared to 1) "submersion," i.e., doing nothing, 2) ESL, i.e., enrollment in a regular classroom with a pullout program of intensive English language instruction for a few hours a week, 3) structured immersion, i.e., enrollment in a self-contained classroom of second-language learners who are taught completely or almost completely in English at a pace they can understand, and 4) bilingual maintenance.

After reviewing the results of these studies, we find no consistent research support for transitional bilingual education as a superior instructional practice for improving the English language achievement of LEP children.

The results varied widely across the 72 studies. When TBE is compared to submersion, the most common finding is no difference in reading and math achievement between students in the two programs. The findings for TBE's effect on language (i.e., writing and knowledge of grammar) are somewhat worse than for TBE's effect on reading. This suggests that students may be less dependent on school for many of the skills learned in reading—decoding, vocabulary, and understanding concepts—than they are for grammar. It appears the fine rules of grammar are learned mostly in school, and, because they are more complex, are more influenced by school time spent on the task. There is, then, a risk that bilingual education students will incur a deficit in learning English grammatical rules because they have spent less time on them than have LEP children in an all-English environment.

One study showed transitional bilingual education produced significantly higher English reading achievement than maintenance bilingual education.[12]

None of the studies comparing reading achievement in TBE to the regular classroom with ESL pullout show TBE to be better. Five studies show no difference between TBE and ESL in reading, and two studies show TBE to be worse than the regular classroom with ESL pullout. Of the three studies that compared language achievement, none showed TBE to be superior, two showed no difference between TBE and ESL, and one showed TBE to be worse.

In developing math proficiency, TBE fared no better when compared to submersion or to regular classroom instruction with ESL pullout.

All but four of the studies of structured immersion compared to TBE or ESL are evaluations of the French immersion programs in English-speaking Canadian provinces, which come in several carefully documented types. When we use the terms "immersion" or "structured immersion" we are talking about the most common program type in Canada—total instruction in the second language during the early grades including learning to read and write in the second language. No studies showed TBE to be superior to structured immersion in reading, language, or math.

Most bilingual education advocates dispute the applicability of the Canadian studies to the United States. First, they argue that the studies are not relevant to the U.S. LEP student experience because the immersion and bilingual education programs in Canada involve mostly middle-class students. In fact, however, several early immersion experiments were conducted with children from low-income families and produced the same or better results.[13] Both the middle-class and poorer English-speaking students who were immersed in French in kindergarten and grade 1 were almost the equal of native-speaking French students until the curriculum became bilingual in grade 2, at which point the French ability of students from English-speaking families declined and continued to decline as English was increased. The time-on-task principle—that is, the amount of time spent learning a subject is the greatest predictor of achievement in that subject—holds across classes in the Canadian programs where school is the only source of second language learning (French) for the native English-speaking children in the bilingual programs.

A second argument made to dismiss the Canadian French immersion experiments is that the students were self-selected. The fact that the students were self-selected means that they were probably better language learners than other students, all other things being equal. Yet, even for these "elite" students, the data show that the time-on-task principle holds. If self-selected students are so influenced by how much time is devoted to a language, it is hard to imagine that LEP children in the United States would not be affected at all.

Contrary to many interpretations of the Canadian experiments,[14] we think there is much we can learn about second language learning from these programs. It is clear, however, that immersion is not a program that can be imported without major modification to fit the U.S. situation where immigrant LEP children arrive at public school every day of the year and must be admitted regardless of their academic preparation.

Advocates of bilingual education have sometimes contended that the issue is learning *in* a language, not learning a language. These data, however, do not show TBE to be superior in either. Moreover, there is no research evidence on the effects of TBE on learning geography, social studies, and history because national standardized achievement tests are not given in these content areas. Any assertions regarding the superiority of TBE in these areas are anecdotal. Moreover, the math findings for TBE suggest an important problem: subject matter is taught in the native tongue, but the student is tested on his or her understanding of that subject *in English.* Many students find it quite difficult to translate into English what was learned in another language in the TBE program. This reduction in achievement caused by the "translation" problem may equal or surpass the reduction in achievement that may occur in the first few months of submersion before the second language is mastered enough to understand subject content.

OTHER RESEARCH REVIEWS

Rossell and Baker (1996) is not the first to show a lack of research support for transitional bilingual education.[15] Given the evidence, on what basis have some reviewers of bilingual education research claimed superiority for the program? One technique, used by Zappert and Cruz (1977), is simply to redefine the word. As they argue,

> No significant difference should not be interpreted as a negative finding for bilingual education...When one adds the fact that students in bilingual education classrooms learn two languages, their native language and a second language, one can conclude that a statistically non-significant finding demonstrates the positive advantages of bilingual education.[16]

The problem with this argument is that the court decisions, the federal regulations, and Chapter 71A are based on the assumption that TBE produces *greater* English language achievement and content area mastery than doing nothing, not the *same* achievement. Doing nothing is considered a violation of a child's equal educational opportunity that transitional bilingual education is supposed to remedy.

Some research reviews make transitional bilingual education appear superior by including performance in Spanish language arts. Zappert and Cruz also do this. While facility in Spanish language arts is important, it is not the goal of government policy nor the stated object of the court decisions.

Interpretations of the same data differ greatly among researchers in the field of bilingual education. Advocates and opponents will frequently interpret data to suit their respective political agendas. Thus, reviewers of the research must carefully read each study and draw their own conclusions.

Second Language Learning Theories

Two competing theories of learning a second language lie at the center of the long debate over the value of transitional bilingual education programs. Proponents of bilingual education programs argue that children should be taught in their native tongue because learning the first language helps them to learn the second language. Critics of bilingual education programs, however, argue that the best way to learn English and subject matter in which one will be evaluated in English is to maximize the time spent hearing, speaking, and writing English. Both theories have problems, although for different reasons, and there is empirical research that appears to contradict each.

The Facilitation Theory

James Cummins is probably the principal proponent of the facilitation theory.[17] Cummins' initial (1978) theoretical work was designed to explain the conflicting findings in the empirical research. The facilitation theory has two components: 1) The "threshold" hypothesis states that a LEP child must attain a high level of linguistic competence in the native tongue before transitioning completely to English in order to avoid cognitive disadvantages. 2) The "developmental interdependence" hypothesis states that the acquisition of a second language is facilitated by reading skills already developed in the first language.

According to the first part of the facilitation theory, if LEP children taught bilingually reach the threshold in their native language, they will be capable of achieving greater proficiency in the second language than students taught entirely in the second language. On the other hand, if a child's bilingual education is abandoned before the threshold in the native language is reached, attainment in the second language will be inferior to that of students taught entirely in the second language. Although the theory is vague regarding the exact level of proficiency in the native language that constitutes the required threshold, the writings of Cumminsimply that it takes considerable time—up to seven years—before the threshold in the native language is attained and the facilitation effect is manifested.

The second part of the facilitation theory claims that once a child has learned to read his or her native language, learning the second language is made easier because he or she has already mastered the "mechanics"—the hardest part—in the native language. Since it takes 3 to 4 years to acquire literacy in roman alphabet languages,[18] the facilitating effect will not become fully apparent until 5 to 7 years after bilingual instruction begins.

It is important to remember that bilingual education preceded the facilitation theory by more than a decade—the former began in 1968 with Title VII of the Elementary and Secondary Education Act and the latter with Cummins' first writing on the subject in 1978.[19] Indeed, the dominant component of second language learning theory in 1968 seems to have been the time-on-task principle. S. Izzo summarizes studies conducted in the late 60s and early 70s:

> The length of time spent in language study is, in fact, one of the most important factors in achievement....[More-over] it must be the total length of time spent in contact with the language that is of importance in determining second language proficiency.[20]

J.B. Carroll goes even further in summarizing the Canadian research evaluations as "eloquent confirmation of the statement that time is the most important factor in learning [a second language]."[21] These conclusions and theories dictated the practice of all-English instruction. Since all-English instruction had not eliminated the achievement differences between Hispanic and white children when the civil rights movement reached its peak in the late 60s, it was replaced by its opposite—native tongue instruction—which, it was argued, would raise the self-esteem and motivation of Hispanic children and ultimately their achievement. The facilitation hypothesis was then created by Cummins and others to provide an educational or linguistic justification for a policy already implemented on civil rights grounds.

Research and the Facilitation Hypothesis

Is the facilitation theory valid? Much of the evidence Cummins cites to demonstrate its validity is either trivial—a study by Cummins and Mulcahy (1977) showing that fluent bilingual Ukrainians did better than either non-fluent bilingual Ukrainians or monolingual students on a test of ambiguities in sentence structure,[22] a study by Leslie (1977) showing that Native American children who scored high on *oral* Cree scored high on English reading[23]—or just plain contrary. Among the latter are studies by Hebert (1976) and Ramirez and Politzer (1976) that show that instruction in the native tongue has no effect on achievement in the second language.[24]

The principal evidence Cummins cites for the effectiveness of transitional bilingual education programs, however, is Skutnabb-Kangas and Toukomaa (1976), who compared two groups of students who had immigrated from Finland to Sweden: those who immigrated before and those who immigrated after reaching the third grade.[25] Students who immigrated after third grade, who had been in school in Finland long enough to have first developed literacy in their native language (Finnish), supposedly performed better in Swedish than did the children who had moved to Sweden at a younger age and who presumably knew less Finnish and began learning Swedish at an earlier age. Both Cummins and Skutnabb-Kangas and Toukomaa argue that the greater ability of these older students in Swedish is a function of more years of instruction in Finnish.

There are major methodological problems with Skutnabb-Kangas and Toukomaa, however, and with the inference that their results support the facilitation hypothesis.[26] First, Skutnabb-Kangas and Toukomaa presented no statistical analysis of their data. Second, at the time of the Skutnabb-Kangas study, Swedish, the second official language of Finland, was a required subject in Finnish schools from the third grade on, a fact neither Skutnabb-Kangas and Toukomaa nor Cummins mention. Thus, if the simple descriptive data presented by Skutnabb-Kangas and Toukomaa show anything, it is that students who have a chance to study a second language before immigrating to the country where that language is spoken perform better than do students who had no such formal instruction before they immigrated. In short, contrary to Cummins' assertions, there is no empirical support in Skutnabb-Kangas and Toukomaa for the facilitation hypothesis and some support for the time-on-task principle.

Other research is sometimes misinterpreted as support for the facilitation hypothesis as well.[27] This research shows 1) that children can transfer skills learned in one language to another language[28] and 2) that older children are, contrary to popular belief, more "efficient" (i.e., faster) learners of languages.[29] Evidence that older learners who already knew how to read in their native language acquired a second language faster than younger learners has been interpreted as support for the facilitation effect.[30] When the proper analysis is conducted, however, the most important causal variable turns out to be age, not native language reading ability.[31] Moreover, while it is true that individuals who are literate in their native language have an easier time learning a second language, this tells us nothing about how nonliterate individuals should be taught, nor in what language.

Perhaps the most important recent test of Cummins' facilitation theory is the Ramirez et al. (1991) national study. This is a methodologically acceptable study with a large national sample of 1,054 students. Although not much discussed in the final report, its design was specifically structured to test Cummins' facilitation theory.[32] The study sampled "early-exit" TBE classrooms, structured immersion, and "late-exit" bilingual maintenance classrooms across the United States. Only the TBE and immersion classrooms were directly compared to each other in statistical analysis.

In the transitional bilingual education and structured immersion program comparisons, Ramirez et al. found at the end of two years (kindergarten to grade one) a significant effect favoring TBE programs in reading, but not in language or math where there was no difference between programs. This advantage of bilingual instruction, however, had vanished by the end of four years in these programs. At that point structured immersion was favored in language arts, while in math and reading there was no significant difference between programs.

While there are enough problems with this study that it should be interpreted with great caution,[33] the fact that the early-exit program did as well as it did in comparison to immersion suggests the following possibility: bilingual education may be superior to all-English instruction in the very beginning when a student literally knows no English, but as the student's English language knowledge increases and English becomes more comprehensible, time on task in English becomes more important and more necessary because it is now *effective* time on task. Ramirez et al., on the other hand, shows *no* support for the facilitation effect. Contrary to the exaggerated claims made, the descriptive portion of the study shows that students who stayed in bilingual education the longest did the worst. While this apparently negative finding for bilingual education is not reliable given the lack of statistical control for student and classroom characteristics, it is definitively *not* positive evidence.

The Burkheimer et al. (1989) study, also funded by the US Department of Education and critiqued by Meyer and Feinberg (1992), shows similar findings. It, too, is a methodologically acceptable study with a large national sample of more than 8,000 students. Not only did it show no facilitation effect, but the only positive effect of any kind from bilingual education in English language arts and math was found in the very beginning of a student's English language acquisition. Although, overall, teaching more English and less Spanish was positively related to achievement in English language arts over a one-year period, this finding varied by initial English proficiency. First graders with greater proficiency in English at the outset tended to improve more when there was more instruction in English. Those who were initially less proficient in English did better with more hours of native language arts instruction.[34]

Instruction in ethnic heritage *decreased* both the overall effect of more English language arts and the relative advantage for those with greater initial English proficiency. This is because as Burkheimer notes (but which is seldom acknowledged by others),

> ...Within a framework that constrains total instructional hours and is further constrained by legislated requirements for some courses, increased instruction in one particular subject area is typically accomplished at the expense of reduction in another subject area...As examples: maintenance of the child's native language skills is accomplished at the expense of reduction in another area; more hours devoted to Ethnic Heritage instruction reduced the remaining hours that could be devoted to other subjects. This reality is not a value judgment of what should or should not be taught (which is best determined by local conditions and goals), but simply a recognition that trade-offs are required (5.42-43).

Finally, the Burkheimer study included a seemingly contradictory finding: having a bilingual certified teacher had a *negative* effect on English language arts achievement for the first grade cohort, but having a teacher who is just familiar with the child's native language had a *positive* effect. It is not clear what this means, but if we assume that being bilingual certified means having a more advanced knowledge of the native tongue than not being bilingual certified, it may mean that some native tongue ability is good, but too much is not. This hypothesis is suggested by other research as well. Fillmore (1980), for example, examined different kinds of bilingual education classes for Chinese students and found that the teacher who was most successful in raising their English language achievement knew Cantonese, the native tongue of most of the students, but taught 90 percent of the time in English.[35] Similarly, the Austin Independent School District's TBE program, found to be superior to submersion, had teachers who used English as the medium of instruction 82 percent of the time.[36]

W. Tickunoff's (1983) descriptive study of successful bilingual instruction (58 teachers from six nationally representative sites) identified the following characteristics of successful programs: 1) 80 percent of time allocated to academic learning tasks, 2) the native tongue used by teachers primarily to clarify instructions, and 3) content areas such as math and social studies taught in *English*.[37] Two studies of the achievement gains of LEP children taught by bilingual and monolingual teachers found no difference between the two.[38] Similarly, the American Institutes for Research (AIR) national survey of bilingual education also found no relationship between whether a teacher was bilingual and the performance of his or her students.[39] Rossell (1990) found no difference in student achievement attributable to whether or not a teacher was bilingual certified.[40]

Moore and Parr (1978) found that teachers in the bilingual education program who were rated *less* competent had better student performance.[41] This finding is not as strange as it sounds if, as seems likely for a bilingual education program, the competence rating is primarily an evaluation of the teacher's ability in the non-English language. What all these studies suggest is that the psychological and perhaps initial pedagogical advantage one may gain from having a teacher fluent in the native tongue may be offset by the tendency of such teachers to teach too much and too long in the native tongue—in other words, to teach according to the facilitation theory.

ENGLISH TIME ON TASK

Opponents of bilingual education programs argue that learning English is determined almost entirely by the time spent studying English.[42] This theory proposes that bilingual education programs are inferior to all-English instruction because bilingual education programs reduce the time spent on the task of learning English.

Any acceptable theory of teaching English to LEP students must account for the contradictory research evidence. Why is it that students in bilingual education programs with up to 30 percent native tongue instruction often do no worse than and sometimes do better than all-English programs? Why is it that monolingual teachers do no better than bilingual teachers?

If time on task were as important as its proponents suggest, all-English instruction would always be superior to any form of bilingual education, even programs where the native tongue is used only in small amounts, and monolingual English teachers would consistently produce greater achievement in their students than bilingual teachers. The scientifically valid studies indicate, however, that this is not the case.

Although some researchers find time on task to be the single greatest predictor of achievement in a subject, it is nevertheless only one of many instructional factors—such as classroom atmosphere, pace of instruction, and curriculum content—that influence academic achievement.[43] Karweit (1983), in a review of the time-on-task literature, concluded that the time-on-task effect, while significant, had been greatly overblown in importance. In reanalyzing the Beginning Teacher Evaluation Study (Fisher et al., 1980), Karweit estimates that an additional 60 minutes per day in time allocated to reading comprehension alone would be needed to increase reading comprehension scores by .25 standard deviations. If that were *effective* time on task, however, only a 10-minute increase would be required to improve mathematics achievement by .25 standard deviations.[44]

As Rossell and Ross (1986) suggested a decade ago, there are some mediating factors for time on task that explain why some methodologically sound research studies show TBE (i.e., less English language time on task) to be no different from or superior to submersion (i.e., more English language time on task). The first of these factors is the nature of the time spent in the English language environment. Much of the learning in a submersion situation is, at least initially, not *effective* learning because the students do not understand what is going on. A bilingual program that gives the children only half their education in English but structures the English so that it is understandable may provide more effective time in the English language than a program that is completely in English if only a small part of it is comprehensible. As English becomes more understandable, the greater time spent on English in the submersion situation would give these children an advantage during this later time period.[45] At the end of three years, students in both submersion and bilingual education may end up with the same amount of effective learning time in the English language, with TBE producing more at the beginning and submersion more at the end.

A second factor explaining the lack of harm of TBE in many good studies is that the supporters of bilingual education may be at least partially right—bilingual education may have important psychological effects that compensate for the reduced English language learning time. If students in submersion programs often feel alienated or inferior, and if a special program is a protected environment that, regardless of its academic utility, makes school more enjoyable, then they may come to school more often, stay longer, and pay more attention. Take, for example, a submersion situation in which students were taught 100 percent in English but only came to school 75 percent of the time, and only half of the instruction was comprehensible in the first year. They will have less effective English language learning time for that year than if they had been in a bilingual program that taught them 50 percent in comprehensible English but motivated them to come to school 85 percent of the time.

Rossell's (1990) comparison in Berkeley, California, of TBE and all-English regular classroom instruction with ESL pullout has some interesting findings that are relevant to this discussion.[46] This study is a methodologically acceptable study of one school district. Rossell found no difference in student achievement between TBE and ESL in the first year's analysis. Interviews with teachers indicated that they used Spanish in the TBE program 30 to 50 percent of the time in kindergarten and first grade and not much after that except for individualized instruction with new non-English-speaking (NEP) students who entered in the later grades. The one TBE program in Berkeley that outperformed all the other school programs, including the regular classroom with ESL pullout programs, had given rise to the original court complaint; it was cited for using too much English. But, contrary to a strict time-on-task theory, the program did have some native tongue instruction.

Rossell conducted a second year evaluation of achievement in the year after the Berkeley Unified School District increased the use of Spanish in its bilingual program in response to pressure from the California State Department of Education. The analysis of the second year found that students in the bilingual program did worse than those in all-English instruction by about 12 to 15 points on reading, language, and math tests. The first year findings, in comparison to those of the second year, suggest some possible explanations: 1) there is some threshold *below* which native tongue instruction does not harm children (the reverse of the facilitation theory), or 2) there is some initial period of time when native tongue instruction actually benefits students. We do not yet have enough evidence to confirm or rule out either possibility, but we can theorize about what is at work here.

Spaced Learning

There is a large body of research on the differential effects of learning material taught at once and continuously versus learning material taught in intervals with rest in between. One classic demonstration of the difference is Duncan (1951) who studied the acquisition of the skill of keeping a pen point on a moving target.[47] One group of subjects practiced for the entire learning time, while the other group was periodically interrupted for rest periods so that they were resting for two-thirds of the practice session. The group with less practice and more rest actually learned better.

A probable explanation for the superiority of spaced practice over continuous practice is that it takes time for the memory process to work. A constant barrage of material to learn overloads the memory process and interferes with learning. Rest, or doing something else between practice sessions, gives the memory process the time it needs to operate, resulting in more efficient learning.

Although learning a language is not exactly the same as learning a boring, repetitive task, there is enough similarity that these studies are suggestive of what might go on in language learning. Consider language learning for the school-aged, monolingual English-speaking child. The child already knows most of the words the teacher uses on any particular day. The few new words to be learned are interspersed with periods of no learning of new words, that is, rest. Language development in the child takes place through spaced, not continuous, practice.

The situation is initially quite different for the child learning a second language. Since all words are new at first, the situation is one of continuous practice. The student may actually make more progress learning the second language if rest is introduced into the constant stream of exposure to the unknown language.

How can rest occur in exposure to a new language? One, although by no means the only, way is to change the language of instruction to one the child already knows. Eventually, enough of the second language will be learned if it is part of the instructional program so that the second language learner will be able to get some "rest" between new words in all-English instruction.[48]

It is possible that bilingual education programs, because they provide a needed rest from constant exposure to the new language, can produce better learning at the early stages of learning a second language. Later on, however, instruction entirely in the second language probably works better than bilingual education, as English is comprehensible enough that new words are a minority.

STUDENT'S SELF-ESTEEM, ATTENDANCE, AND ATTITUDES ABOUT SCHOOL

Advocates of bilingual education and bilingual teachers have argued that examining the effect of these program features on the academic achievement of students is too limited an analysis. They argue that bilingual education programs and bilingual teachers have a positive psychological effect on their students that is important in and of itself. Many of the teachers who teach in bilingual education programs believe that the purpose of these programs is to improve the self-esteem of children and by so doing improve their academic achievement. Despite the popularity of this theory, we could find very little research on this subject, scientific or otherwise.

CONCLUSION

The facilitation hypothesis has been overwhelmingly accepted by educators in bilingual education as a proven fact and as the explanation for TBE's superiority to all other second language acquisition techniques, even though more than 15 years of research and literally thousands of studies have confirmed neither the theory nor the predicted effectiveness of bilingual education programs. Unfortunately, the latest scientifically designed research project, the Ramirez et al. (1991) study, costing millions of dollars, has made only a small contribution to our understanding of this issue. If anything, the Ramirez et al. (1991) and Burkheimer et al. (1989) studies suggest to us that the threshold theory may work in reverse of Cummins' hypothesis. It seems more likely that a threshold in the second language, not the native language, needs to be passed before the second language instruction is consistently superior to native language instruction. Indeed, native language skills (after controlling for intelligence, something almost no one does) could be *irrelevant* to this process.

CHAPTER FOUR

EVERY CLASSROOM IS AN ISLAND: THE IMPLEMENTATION OF TBE IN MASSACHUSETTS SCHOOLS

How has Chapter 71A been implemented in Massachusetts? What does transitional bilingual education look like as it is actually practiced in the schools and classrooms in the state? Who are the students enrolled? The answers to these questions come from several sources, including state and federal documents, classroom observations, and interviews with educators and administrators.

MASSACHUSETTS COMPARED TO OTHER STATES

In comparison to other states and to the country as a whole, Massachusetts has a relatively large percentage of language minority students—that is, children who speak a language other than English (U.S. Census definition)[1] or, in Massachusetts, someone whose first language is not English.[2] In the United States in 1990 only 4 percent of the five- to 17-year-old population was language minority; in Massachusetts the figure was 12 percent.[3]

LEP (limited-English-proficient) students are a subset of language minority students—only about half of all language minority students are classified as LEP by the time they enter school. Figure 4-1 and appendix 4-1 show the percentage of public school students classified as LEP in the United States as a whole and in the several states with the largest percentage classified as LEP.

According to these statistics, Massachusetts is among the top 10 states in the percentage of all public school students classified as

LEP. LEP students in the United States are concentrated in two areas: the west and the northeast. No southern states are in the top 10, and only one midwestern state—Illinois, largely because of Chicago—is in this category.

Figure 4–1
% of Public School Students Classified as LEP in Top 10 States and U.S. Average and Total %, 1991–1992

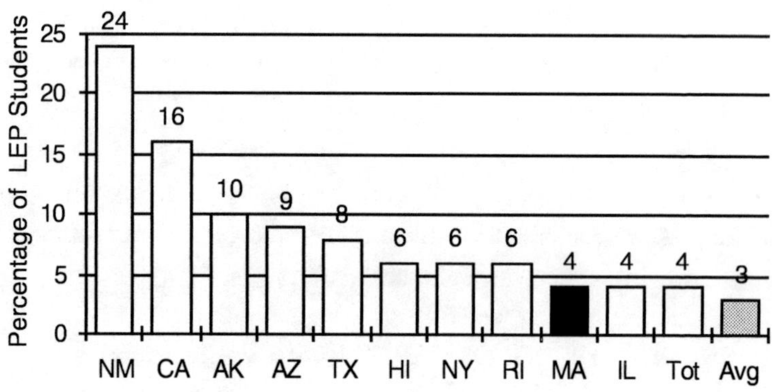

Source: American Legislative Exchange Council (ALEC) and U.S. English Foundation, *Bilingual Education in the United States 1991-92, Special Supplement, The Report Card on American Education 1994*, Washington, D.C., 1994:6-7; American Legislative Exchange Council (ALEC), *Report Card on American Education 1994: A State-by-State Analysis*, Washington, D.C., 1994:40-41.
Note: Total percentage is the percent in the United States as a whole. Average percentage is the average across all states.

There is another way to look at these data, and that is to ask what percentage of the total LEP population in the United States is contained in each state. Figure 4-2 shows the 12 states that enroll 90 percent of the LEP population in the United States ranked by the percentage each enrolls. California, by virtue of its sheer size and proximity to Mexico, contains 43 percent of the public school LEP population in the United States. Texas is second with 15 percent. Massachusetts, with 2 percent of the total, ranks ninth in its share of the LEP student population in the United States.

Figure 4–2
% of LEP Students in U.S. by State, 1991–1992

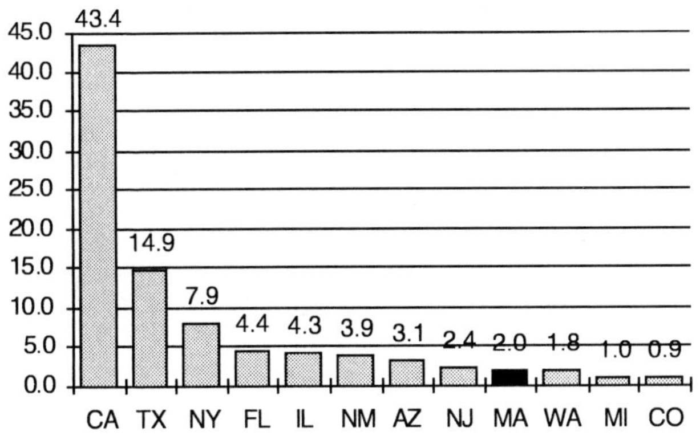

Source: American Legislative Exchange Council (ALEC) and U.S. English Foundation, *Bilingual Education in the United States 1991-92*, Special Supplement, *The Report Card on American Education 1994*, Washington, D.C., 1994:6-7.
Note: These 12 states contain 90 percent of the LEP students in the United States.

The number or percentage of students considered LEP is a function not only of the number of language minority students in a state but of the policies and procedures used to classify students as LEP (see chapter 5). These procedures vary from state to state and school district to school district. In Massachusetts, according to the data shown in figure 4-3, 51 percent of the language minority students in the 51 TBE districts (districts that had more than 20 of a single language minority group and thus were in the TBE reports) are classified as LEP.

Figure 4-3
% Each Language Minority Group Classified as LEP in Massachusetts, 1992–1993

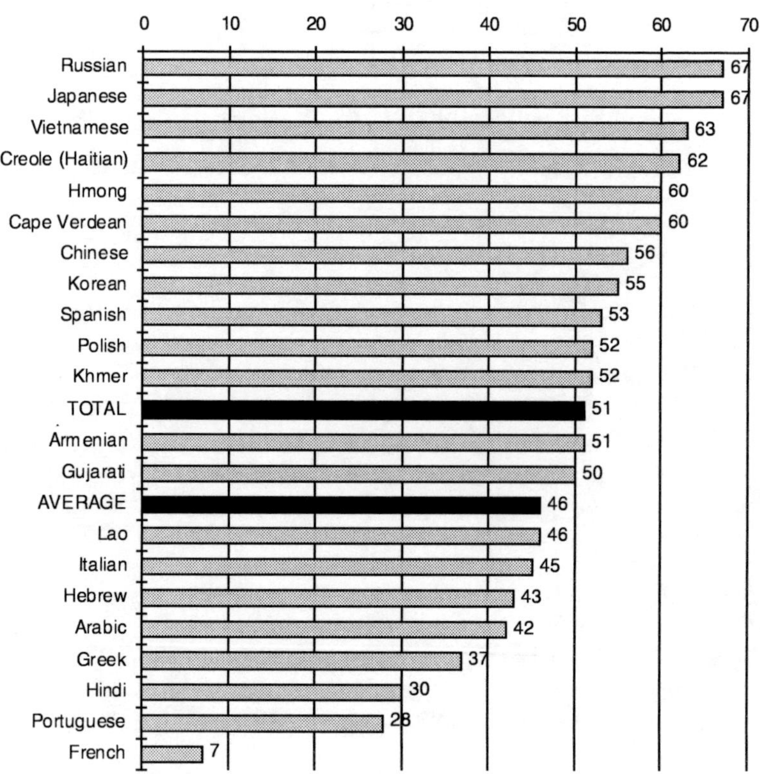

Source: Massachusetts Department Of Education, *Transitional Bilingual Education Report for the Year Ending June 30,1993*, table 2.

Note: This includes only language minority groups with more than 100 students. Language minority is defined as those children whose first language is not English. Massachusetts data for 1993–1994 were not available when this book went to press.

The Predominance of Spanish Speakers Among LEPs

Spanish speakers represent the largest single language minority group in the LEP population. Spanish speakers represented 73 percent of the U.S. LEP population in 1991-92 and 58 percent of the 1992-93 Massachusetts LEP population.[4] In the United States, the next largest group after Spanish is Vietnamese at 4 percent of the total LEP population. In Massachusetts, the next largest groups are Khmer, Portuguese, Chinese, and Vietnamese, all at 6 percent of the total LEP population in the entire state.

There are several possible explanations for the predominance of Spanish speakers among LEP students. First, Spanish speakers in Massachusetts are mainly immigrants from Latin America, who tend to be poorer and less educated than immigrants from other areas of the world and thus statistically more likely than other groups to fail a criterion test that requires educational skills.[5]

Second, the United States shares a long border with a Spanish-speaking country, and large communities are able to form in which a child, while born in this country, can spend five preschool years without hearing much English at all. While this can certainly happen in any immigrant community, the likelihood increases with the size of the concentration in a single geographic area. (This may also explain why Spanish speakers are a lower percentage of LEP students in Massachusetts than in the country as a whole—the lack of a common border with a Spanish-speaking country reduces the size of Spanish-speaking communities and increases the likelihood of coming into contact with English speakers and of learning English before entering school.)

Third, as the largest single language group in the United States, Spanish speakers have the numbers to fill self-contained classrooms using the native tongue as a medium of instruction. There may be a lot of Spanish speakers in the LEP population simply because there is a program for them.

But not all Spanish speakers are LEP. As shown in figure 4-3, in Massachusetts in 1992-93, only 53 percent of those whose first language is Spanish were classified as LEP, while two-thirds of Russian speakers and Japanese speakers were classified as LEP. In Massachusetts Spanish speakers are more likely to be born in this country than are Russian or Japanese speakers and more likely to have learned English. If we look at this by census grouping rather than language, in Massachusetts one-third of all Hispanic students five to 17 years old are classified as LEP, and in the United States 36 percent are classified as LEP.[6]

ENROLLMENT IN TBE PROGRAMS IN MASSACHUSETTS

Federal and state laws, regulations, and court orders affect both the classification of students as LEP and their enrollment in TBE programs. Appendix 4-1 shows the results of a national survey of LEP student enrollment in different education programs. These results are unfortunately biased by the fact that they count only LEP students enrolled in programs that were identified and funded at the state or local level. The program alternatives were 1) bilingual, 2) regular classroom enrollment with ESL pullout, or 3) "unknown." Compare the first column, labeled "Bilingual," to the fourth column, which contains the total number of LEP students. All of Massachusetts' LEP students are enrolled in bilingual education according to this survey. This is also true of Alaska, Minnesota, New Mexico, and Hawaii. This does not mean, however, that all LEP students are in TBE, nor does it mean that all LEP students in TBE are receiving native tongue instruction. The funding incentive is to identify as "bilingual" more programs than actually use native tongue instruction. This survey shows that 60 percent of LEP students in the United States are enrolled in nominally bilingual programs and 40 percent in ESL or "unknown" programs. The average state enrolls 30 percent of its LEP students in nominally bilingual programs.

Figure 4-4 shows the 1992-93 percentage each language minority group comprised of the Massachusetts TBE population. These data come from the *Transitional Bilingual Education Report* for 1992-93 in the 51 TBE school districts. Since the only school districts in the state with programs called TBE are the 51 TBE districts, their data represent TBE enrollment and characteristics for the whole state.

Figure 4–4
% Each Language Minority Group is of Massachusetts TBE Enrollment, 1992–1993

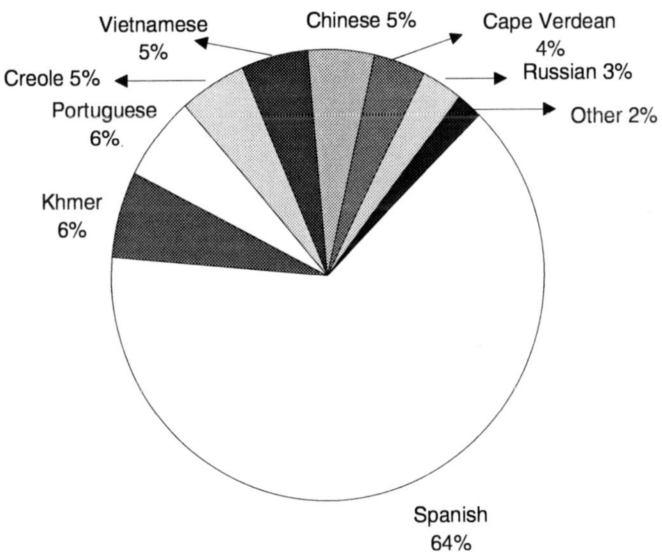

Source: Massachusetts Department of Education, *Transitional Bilingual Education Report for Year Ending June 30,1993*, table 2.

These 51 districts, shown in appendix 4-2, in 1994-5, enrolled 91 percent of the Hispanic students, 96 percent of the Spanish language minority students, and 98 percent of the Spanish-speaking LEP students in the state. Spanish speakers are 64 percent of the state's TBE enrollment, and there is no other single language minority group with nearly as large a percentage. The next largest groups are Khmer speakers and Portuguese speakers at 6 percent each of the state TBE enrollment. Haitian Creole speakers, Vietnamese speakers, and "Chinese" speakers[7] are each 5 percent of the state's TBE enrollment. Cape Verdeans and Russian speakers are next at 4 and 3 percent respectively. All the other language minority groups enrolled in programs called TBE together represent only 2 percent of the state's TBE population. As this data and appendix 4-3 suggest, only the Spanish speakers have sufficient numbers for a self-contained program of native tongue instruction at each grade level.

Figure 4-5 shows the percentage of each LEP group enrolled in programs called TBE in the 51 TBE districts in Massachusetts in 1992-93. This figure is confined to language minority groups with more than 100 LEP students in the entire state. Despite the fact that Spanish speakers are less likely to be classified as LEP than are Russian, Japanese, Vietnamese, Haitian Creole, Hmong, Cape Verdean, "Chinese," or Korean speakers, the sheer size of the group results in 81 percent of the Spanish-speaking LEP students being enrolled, slightly greater than the Khmer population (79 percent) and the Portuguese population (72 percent). The average percentage of a single language group enrolled is 12 percent. Across all LEP language minority groups (not just those with more than 100 LEP students), only 37 percent are enrolled in programs called TBE.

Figure 4-5
% of Each LEP Group
Enrolled in TBE in Massachusetts, 1992–1993

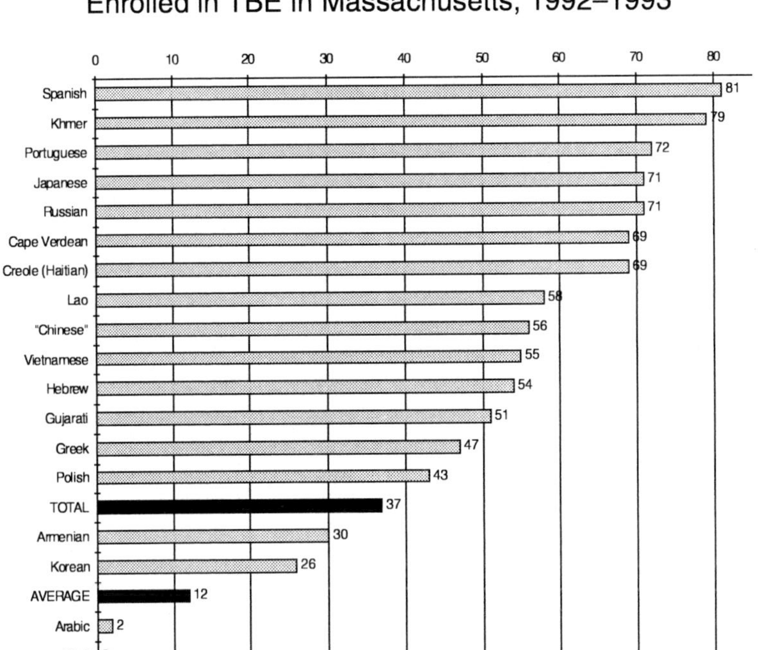

Source: Massachusetts Department of Education, *Transitional Bilingual Education Report for the Year Ending June 30, 1993*, table 2.
Note: This includes only language minority groups with more than 100 students in the state.

Figure 4-6 shows the total TBE enrollment for 1992-93 in Massachusetts in the 15 districts with the largest number of TBE students. Boston has by far the largest enrollment, capturing 31 percent of the 38,636 students enrolled in Massachusetts TBE programs. Lawrence is next with 10 percent, Lowell has 8 percent, Springfield 7 percent, and Holyoke 6 percent of the TBE students in the 51 TBE districts.

The next 10 districts all have less than 5 percent each; these 15 districts cumulatively enroll 86 percent of the state's total TBE population.

Figure 4-6
The 15 Districts in Massachusetts with the Largest Share of TBE Students, 1992–1993

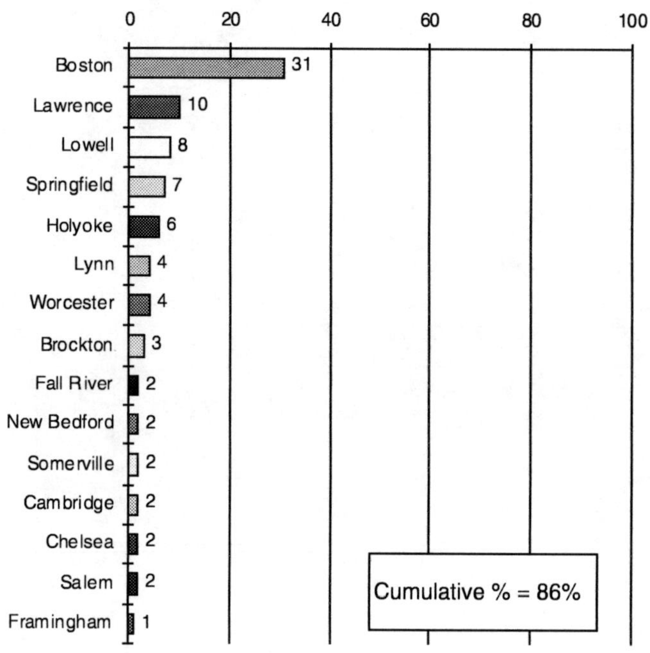

Source: Massachusetts Department of Education, *Transitional Bilingual Education Report for Year Ending June 30,1993*, table 1.
Note: The percentage is the percentage of all 38,636 TBE students in Massachusetts in 1992-1993 enrolled in that district.

We can also look at these statistics in terms of the extent to which each district is dominated by TBE students. Figure 4-7 shows the top 15 TBE districts in Massachusetts in terms of the percentage of each district's total student population enrolled in TBE. Below that bar is the percentage Hispanic of each district. The correlation between the percentage of students enrolled in TBE and the percentage of students who are Hispanic is 0.81 across all districts, highly statistically significant.

The rankings in figures 4-6 and 4-7 are slightly different from each other because the former rankings partly reflect the size of the city. We would expect that the larger the city, the larger its share of the state's TBE population, and this is pretty much what figure 4-6 shows. Figure 4-7, by contrast, indicates which districts are dominated by TBE students regardless of size. No school district has more than 40 percent of its students enrolled in TBE, and the average is 7 percent.

Lawrence leads the way with 37 percent of its total students enrolled in TBE, although because it is smaller than Boston it has a smaller share of the state's TBE enrollment. The district with the next largest percentage of students enrolled in TBE is Holyoke at 31 percent. These two school districts are overwhelmingly Hispanic, with Lawrence being three-quarters and Holyoke being 67 percent Hispanic. Lowell ranks third with 22 percent of its students enrolled in TBE programs, roughly equal to the size of its Hispanic population. Boston is fourth among Massachusetts school districts with only 19 percent of its students enrolled in TBE programs, although it has 31 percent of the state's TBE population. Although Boston is the largest city in Massachusetts and has an 82 percent minority public school enrollment, its Hispanic enrollment is only 24 percent.

Figure 4-7
The 15 Districts with the Largest Percentage of Total Student Enrollment in TBE, 1992–1993

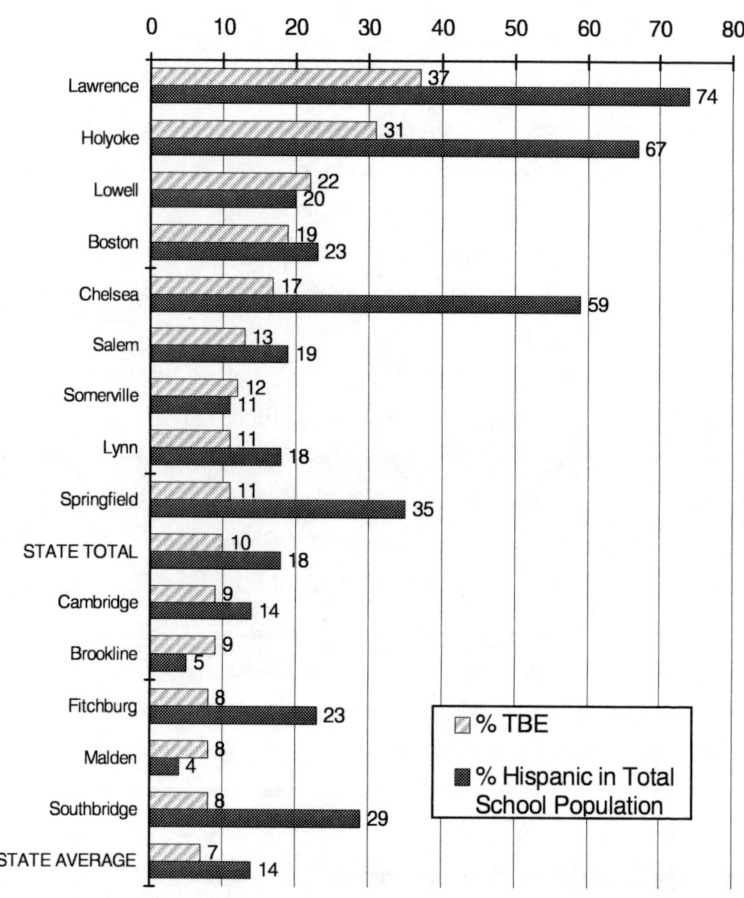

Source: Massachusetts Department Of Education, *Transitional Bilingual Education Report for Year Ending June 30,1993*, table 1; and Massachusetts Department of Education, Office of Planning Research and Evaluation, Individual School Report, October 1, 1992.
Note: The percentage TBE is the percentage of all students in that district who were in TBE in 1992-1993.

These TBE enrollment figures do not guarantee, of course, that students are actually receiving native tongue instruction. Although program enrollment figures are suggestive in that one can generally assume that programs smaller than 100 at the elementary level (K-5) do not include native tongue instruction and that secondary programs only have native tongue instruction in one or two subjects, even these generalizations must be confirmed by talking to administrators and teachers in each district or by observing classes.

Classroom Observations

Our notion that there is no such thing as a single bilingual education treatment in this state comes in part from observations of more than 75 classrooms at all grade levels and in nine language groups in Massachusetts over the last two years.[8] These observations are supplemented by extensive discussions with TBE teachers, ESL teachers, principals, directors of TBE, administrators in these school districts, discussions with state department of education employees, and the results of a survey of the 51 TBE school districts conducted by the Massachusetts Executive Office of Education in the spring of 1993.

The purpose of these observations was to identify factors that appear to determine how closely the education program followed the model approved by the state and mandated in state legislation. The classroom observations have been summarized in this chapter by language group. Distinguishing programs by language group is important not only in Massachusetts where native tongue instruction is required but in the United States as a whole. There are significant differences between these groups in 1) the political pressure to use the native tongue in education programs, 2) the availability of teachers and written materials, and 3) size, which affects the ability of school districts to fill a classroom with a single language group. A sample of the observations made from the classroom visits will illustrate the variety in classroom focus and the range of teacher qualifications and attitudes within and between the various TBE programs.

SPANISH

While Spanish language TBE programs most closely approximate the mandated model, even they are by no means uniform, varying across districts, across schools, and across classrooms within schools. There are almost 30,000 Spanish-speaking LEP students in 44 of the TBE districts. Thirty-six districts have more than 20 Spanish-speaking LEP students, and 24 districts have more than 130 LEP students—on average enough to fill a classroom by combining two grades.[9]

In one kindergarten class we visited, a bilingual teacher and two Spanish-speaking aides teach 22 Spanish-speaking students entirely in Spanish. Although some students are also comfortable in English, it is not used in instruction at all during the period of observation.

In a second kindergarten class, the bilingual teacher teaches in both languages because she has one student who speaks more English than Spanish. Her aide speaks to the students only in Spanish, however.

In a third kindergarten class, the bilingual teacher teaches in both languages, with emphasis on Spanish. The teacher's understanding is that the purpose of kindergarten is to offer a positive education experience, reinforce the Spanish language skills of the students, and not necessarily to acquaint them with the English-speaking world.

In a fourth kindergarten class, English is taught for 15 minutes each day. By the end of the year, students have been taught 200 English words, roughly the vocabulary of a two-year-old child. This teacher also believes that creating a happy learning environment is her primary goal.

In a fifth kindergarten class, there are several students who are Hispanic but whose strongest language is English, according to their teacher. They are nonetheless taught entirely in Spanish, translated into English only occasionally.

In the first grade classrooms the theory behind TBE can be more clearly observed. Most classroom teachers teach their Spanish-speaking students to read and write in Spanish. Only when they are proficient in Spanish will they be transitioned to English. A few teachers do teach English reading and writing as well but they understand that they are violating the theory. Classroom walls are covered with Spanish language materials. In one first grade class, the teacher has been increasing spoken English over the course of the year. The students appear to understand what is said fairly well, but cannot read, write, or speak English at all well. When asked, this teacher says she does not believe her students could have learned as well or better in English and mentions as evidence for her assertion that the Khmer-speaking LEP students taught entirely in English fall behind in their subjects. She emphasizes that teaching her students to read in Spanish enables their parents to help them with their reading at home, as well as other homework—a point also made in a national study of bilingual education programs.[10] She expects her students, many of whom were in a Spanish-only kindergarten, to be reading in English by the end of second grade and mainstreamed by the end of third grade. This means these students will have been in TBE for four years rather than three, as the law stipulates.

One second grade class had been taught for several months by an ESL teacher substituting for the TBE teacher who had left. She said her students had made great progress toward fluency in English. Although few had any English skills at the start of the year, by mid-year, all were reading, writing, and speaking English. When a new TBE teacher took over the class, he delivered all instruction in Spanish because that was the language in which he was most comfortable. The ESL teacher then had one and one-half hours each day in which to continue the English language instruction. She expressed her frustration with a system that rigidly emphasized Spanish language proficiency as the key to academic success.

In one third grade class, a bilingual teacher and a Spanish-speaking aide teach using the "concurrent method." In practice this means going back and forth between two languages with the goal of students' reading and writing in both. As might be expected this goal is very difficult to achieve. The teacher acknowledges that all teachers find it difficult to teach two languages at once and that many students are having trouble; she has three students who have virtually no reading skills, and, although most of the students have been in the school and a bilingual classroom since first grade, few are fluent in English.

In another third grade class, there appears to be no attempt to transition the students to English. All instruction is in Spanish, and all materials, except a math book, are in Spanish as well.

In a different third grade class, the amount of English language instruction depends on whether or not the students are expected to be mainstreamed the following year. If so, they receive two hours of instruction in English each day. If not, they receive only one hour and 15 minutes.

A fourth grade math class is taught entirely in Spanish, even though most of the students are fluent in English. One student is not, however, and so the teacher uses the language that *all* the students understand.

In a combined fourth and fifth grade TBE class, students are taught English grammar entirely in English with English materials. The TBE instructor's English, however, is poor, and he makes several serious grammatical errors during the lesson.

In one fifth grade class the focus is on developing skills in both languages. The teacher reports that the parents of these students want them to learn English, and so she tries to teach mostly in English. She also believes the law requires her to use a lot of English and that the sole reason for using Spanish is to show respect for the native culture and raise the students' self-esteem.

A combined fifth and sixth grade math class is taught mostly in Spanish by a teacher who failed the Spanish certifying exam, apparently because he did not grasp the fine points of Spanish grammar. Although he is certified to teach math, he is on a waiver as a TBE teacher. Were it not for the shortage of TBE teachers, he would not be allowed to teach at all.

Several sixth grade teachers who teach primarily in English explain that they teach Spanish literacy because they want their students to maintain their Spanish skills. But they make it clear that their primary goal is English proficiency and that students will only learn English if they are taught in English. Another teacher said she believes students will get jobs because of their Spanish and not their English skills. Her class consisted of some students about to be mainstreamed and some who spoke no English whatsoever. Two chalkboards contained the same science lesson, in English on one and in Spanish on another.

One sixth grade social studies class is considered a two-way bilingual program. All the students are fluent in English; some are fluent in Spanish. They are all taking Spanish as a foreign language. In this class, all instruction is in English. In the Spanish class, the teacher teaches the native Spanish speakers in Spanish and the native English speakers in English. He gives almost no homework because he does not know how to bridge the gap in Spanish language knowledge between the two groups.

A Spanish TBE and ESL teacher in one district has a pullout program designed to bring students up to speed in English. She is appalled by the number of students she sees who have had little or no English instruction. She believes that only a special needs student would have trouble learning English in a regular classroom with the support of ESL pullout. She also believes that not all children can be bilingual and that, contrary to TBE theory, the children with learning problems are least able to be truly bilingual and should not be taught to read and write in Spanish.

A seventh grade basic skills class is taught in Spanish, although most students understand English. The teacher estimates that 90 percent of these students will not graduate from high school, and 50 percent will go into special education classes.

A seventh grade two-way Spanish bilingual class is taught in a mixture of Spanish and English. The teacher sees the main goal of the two-way program as teaching the Hispanic students English.

An eighth grade teacher of science and math teaches completely in Spanish, and students are mainstreamed for classes they can handle in English. Most of these students have been in this country less than two years and are two or three grade levels behind in their own language. They will probably be taught in Spanish in one or more classes for five years. The teacher believes the two most important determinants of whether students are ready to be mainstreamed are their motivation and their skills in the language arts of their native tongue, not English. He does plan to increase their exposure to English by switching to an English-language algebra textbook because he worries about how little English they are getting in the TBE program and in his class.

A high school algebra class for ninth and tenth graders is taught by a woman who was an engineer in Puerto Rico. She has neither a regular nor a bilingual teaching certificate. She teaches the class entirely in Spanish, and our conversation reveals that her English is not fluent and probably not adequate for teaching algebra in English.

An American history class is also taught completely in Spanish by a teacher without a certificate and is taught from an American values perspective emphasizing liberalism, individualism, freedom, autonomy, and independence. When asked in English, one student could not answer simple questions regarding her age, grade, or how long she had been in the United States, although she had been enrolled in the school for nine months.

The teacher of a General Math class, who teaches entirely in Spanish, made it clear that for his students the goal was a high school degree and not English proficiency. Most were from Puerto Rico, had been in Massachusetts less than two years, and had poor English skills. Indeed, even those who had been in the state several years had poor English skills.

From these and other observations some tentative conclusions can be drawn about the Spanish language TBE programs in Massachusetts: There is native tongue instruction in self-contained classrooms with students learning to read and write in Spanish and gradually transitioning to English. There are also Spanish TBE programs with very little native language instruction, although these occur primarily in districts with small numbers of Spanish-speaking LEP students. Whenever there are enough Spanish speakers to fill a classroom—and the Spanish speakers are more likely than other groups to have the numbers to fill a classroom—they usually receive native language instruction. One striking difference between the Spanish-speaking population and other language groups (see below) is that many fluent Spanish speakers are non-native speakers. The labor pool of bilingual teachers (speaking English and Spanish) is thus increased by the availability of non-native speakers, a resource no other TBE program has available.

Spanish TBE teachers have widely varying attitudes about the purpose of the program, and these differences are reflected in how class time is spent. Their attitudes may be formed from experience, by guidelines laid out by administrators, or by exposure to bilingual education research. For example, one fourth grade teacher attributed her continued attempts to perfect the Spanish language skills of her students to a course she is taking at Boston University. Based on this course she believes that a "thorough literature review" revealed that "the highest possible literacy skills in Spanish lead to the highest possible literacy skills in English." The same teacher has experience teaching English to adult immigrants and has found that those who are literate in their native language have an easier time learning English. From this experience she has concluded that students should first acquire literacy in the native language.

The flaws in this logic are clear: one cannot assume that because there is a correlation between two factors that the most efficient remedy for a deficit in one factor is an increase in the other. Another likely explanation for this teacher's experience with adult immigrants is that the educational problems that have prevented an adult from gaining literacy in the native language will also inhibit the acquisition of a second language.

Some general principles also emerged from these observations: Teachers tend to teach in the language that most students understand (if they are fluent in that language themselves). In pre-school and elementary programs, the language of instruction depends on the makeup of the classroom and the language proficiency of the instructor. If all the students are Spanish speakers, instruction is in Spanish. If there are non-Spanish speakers in the classroom and all the students understand English, instruction is primarily in English. Teachers' aides may speak and assist in the primary language of instruction or in the other language depending on the help particular students need. They may translate English instruction into Spanish or Spanish instruction into English or simply reinforce the instruction given.

Cape Verdean (Kriolu)

Unlike Spanish, Cape Verdean (Kriolu) is not an official language anywhere in the world (Portuguese is the official language of Cape Verde). Kriolu is an oral not a written language, and it is U.S. academics who have only recently constructed a written language for the purpose of running TBE programs in Massachusetts. There are 2,230 Cape Verdean LEP students in 18 TBE districts in Massachusetts, five of which have 20 or more Cape Verdean LEP students. Two districts have more than 130 students. There are few non-native speakers, few bilingual teachers, and a lack of appropriate materials for instruction in the native language. There is considerable disagreement within the Cape Verdean community whether efforts should be made to ensure native tongue instruction. Further complicating the issue are the number of different dialects spoken on the islands. A teacher cannot be sure that the dialect she speaks will be understood by all the students in her classroom. The net result is even if there are enough Cape Verdean LEP students to fill a classroom, the students we observed learn to read and write in English, not in any Cape Verdean dialect.

In one kindergarten classroom, 18 Cape Verdean students are taught entirely in English, with only occasional use of the native tongue to emphasize a concept. The students speak in both languages; all materials on the walls and instructional materials are in English, with the exception of teacher-constructed materials designed to acknowledge Cape Verdean culture. Students headed to first grade will either be mainstreamed or go to a different school if their parents choose to continue the TBE program. Parents have the right to withdraw their child after kindergarten, but the teachers do not recommend it until they have been in it for three and sometimes four or five years.

The teacher estimated that 85 percent of her students will continue in the TBE program, which is conducted almost entirely in English.

A first grade class and a second grade class in a different school follow the same pattern—English instruction with only occasional native tongue clarification. The first grade teacher asserts that all students who began in September are completely fluent in English by June.

HAITIAN CREOLE

There are about 3,000 Haitian Creole LEP students in 21 TBE districts. Nine districts have more than 20 students, and three districts have more than 150 students. Like Cape Verdean, Haitian Creole is not the official language of a large country or area, and there are few written materials available. Although the official languages of Haiti are French and Creole, there are few textbooks in Creole and even fewer exported to the United States. Teachers must construct any Haitian Creole materials themselves, and, as a result, do so only for cultural enrichment. Instruction we observed in elementary Haitian Creole TBE programs is generally in English, with English textbooks and workbooks.

In one first grade class, the teacher uses Creole only to help a student who has just recently arrived in the United States. She claims it takes the average student at most *three or four months* to understand enough English for every lesson to be a learning experience. She sees the TBE program as a bridge between the Creole-speaking home and the English-speaking school, and she neither cares about nor believes in the theory behind transitional bilingual education. Her goal is to help students feel comfortable in the classroom and prepare them for the day they will leave the program to go into a regular classroom. As she puts it, they must be instructed in English because they cannot stay in the bilingual program forever.

A fifth grade Haitian Creole TBE class consists of some students who have had no previous schooling, some who have been to school in Haiti, and some who have had some schooling in the United States. The teacher said he teaches the students without previous schooling to read and write in Creole with Creole textbooks, although he did not have any Creole textbooks in the classroom. He speaks a mixture of English and Creole to the class to accommodate the one student who has just arrived from Haiti. All but this one student speak English, are being taught in English, and converse informally in English.

Two high school classes were observed. In the first, a social science class, the teacher teaches almost entirely in Creole but uses English materials. Eleven of twelve students are male; several appear to be asleep. This school's program includes native language classes in Creole grammar, math, social studies, science, and one English class. Apparently, the goal of the program is to graduate the students and only secondarily to teach them English. In the second class, a math class, instruction is again in Creole using English materials, and most of the students are male. It seems that the TBE program at this school is primarily a dropout prevention program. The teacher refuses to permit the students to be questioned as to how long they have been in the United States because he says they would not answer for fear of "getting into trouble."

The elementary and secondary programs for this language group can differ considerably. At the elementary level, students we observed are taught almost completely in English in order to prepare them for the regular English language classroom. At the secondary level, students we observed are taught completely in Creole in the hopes of keeping them from dropping out of school.

JAPANESE

There are only about 230 Japanese LEP students in 12 TBE districts in Massachusetts, too few in any single district to have self-contained bilingual classrooms, although the law requires the four that have more than 20 to maintain a TBE program, even at 1 to 2 Japanese students per grade in a classroom. Although most Japanese families in the programs intend to return to Japan, and so might be expected to want native tongue instruction, Japanese parents generally consider an all-English classroom to be their child's best opportunity to learn English, a prestigious international language.

Japanese-speaking students we observed are taught entirely in English in a regular classroom with pullout help as needed. In one school, the Japanese TBE teacher has two small resource rooms and two aides. The emphasis in this pullout program is on learning English. The TBE teacher is a resource for the Japanese LEP students and the regular classroom teacher. She maintains a library of books and learning materials in Japanese for students to take home and read alone or with their parents. She goes into classrooms at the request of the regular teacher and gives special assignments, such as keeping a daily journal in Japanese, to students who have not yet learned English but who are literate in Japanese. She also assists students with regular class work by providing translation as necessary or simply extra help. She does not teach Japanese to any student.

The Japanese kindergarten children in this program are in a difficult situation if their parents do return to Japan, however, as they learn no Japanese whatsoever. The TBE teacher recommends that parents spend time teaching their children Japanese at home or enroll them in a Saturday Japanese school. In sum, the Japanese transitional bilingual education programs we observed are not bilingual, but simply a resource for Japanese LEP students and their parents.

VIETNAMESE

There are about 3,500 Vietnamese LEP students in 36 TBE districts in Massachusetts. Sixteen districts have more than 20 Vietnamese LEP students, and six have more than 130.

The only country where Vietnamese is spoken is Vietnam, there are few written materials, and immigrants to the United States are mostly political refugees with no intention of returning. In every classroom observed, all published materials were in English, with a few teacher-constructed materials in Vietnamese.

In the entire K-6 elementary program in this school, there are 38 Vietnamese LEP students, only 12 in grades 1 through 3. The first classroom observed was a kindergarten TBE class of 22 students. This kindergarten teacher teaches in English with occasional translation into Vietnamese; she has an aide who speaks only English. All instructional materials are in English, and students speak to each other in both languages. The teacher is using kindergarten as a transition into an English-speaking first grade class. She views her job as making sure the students learn English in a supportive environment that will motivate them to excel academically in a regular all-English classroom. She has no desire to maintain Vietnamese nor to develop reading and writing in Vietnamese, nor has she been educated in the theory behind transitional bilingual education.

The Vietnamese TBE program continues through grade 3, but there is little native tongue instruction. The small number of students makes it impossible to fill self-contained classrooms. This district claims to offer five content area classes in Vietnamese at the high school level. There are, however, only 69 LEP Vietnamese students in these grades, and so there is probably little native tongue instruction, particularly as there are few or no instructional materials in Vietnamese.

KHMER (CAMBODIAN)

There are about 3,000 Khmer-speaking LEP students in 28 TBE districts. Thirteen have more than 20 Khmer-speaking students, and five have more than 130. There is great difficulty finding certified teachers who can teach in Khmer, which uses a non-Roman alphabet, is difficult to learn, and bears no resemblance to English. A student who learns to read in Khmer, unlike a student who learns to read in Spanish—a language that uses the Roman alphabet—has to learn the skills of deciphering characters and pronouncing words all over again to read and write in English. Not surprisingly, in the Khmer programs observed, students learn to read and write in English.

In one Khmer classroom visited, a combined kindergarten and first grade TBE class consists of 14 students (the district has 55 LEP Khmer speakers in grades K-6). The students are learning to read and write in English, with only occasional translation into Khmer. The teacher uses English materials and sees her job as preparing the students for an all-English classroom. The school does have a combined first and second grade TBE class, so some students may continue in the program, while others are mainstreamed.

Another kindergarten class has 18 students and a teacher that speaks no Khmer, although an aide in the classroom does. All instruction is in English, all materials are in English, but some students speak to each other in Khmer. It is the end of the year, and all students who began in September can now speak English, although some may still be more comfortable speaking in Khmer.

A combined first and second grade TBE class consists of 16 students. The district's program continues through grade 4 with a combined third and fourth grade class taught in English with Khmer enrichment and translation. Students in these classes are taught the Khmer alphabet, but none of the teachers believe that learning to read and write in Khmer will assist students in learning English. Nor do they expect that students will ever learn content areas in Khmer, as it would take years of studying Khmer to enable them to comprehend textbooks. The purpose of the Khmer curriculum is cultural enrichment and increased self-esteem. Other classrooms exhibit this same pattern—students are taught to read and write in English, and then simple words in the native language are added. Some schools have Khmer pullout programs for adding Khmer language and cultural enrichment to an all-English program in the later grades.

The Khmer TBE programs we visited operate in exactly the reverse of TBE theory—they learn English first, and then the native tongue is added. Teachers either do not know the theory behind TBE, or they dismiss it because they are certain that learning Khmer will not help students learn English. When asked about the effect of the time spent on Khmer in the later grades, one teacher acknowledged that it probably held students back because it took away from the time they had to study English and their other subjects. She attributed the continued efforts at teaching Khmer to the requirements of the state department of education and perceived the state's intention to be improving students' self-esteem through acknowledgment of their cultural heritage.

GREEK

The population of Greek-speaking LEP students in Massachusetts is small—about 400 in 19 TBE districts. Only three districts have more than 20 Greek LEP students, only one has more than 130. This language does not use the Roman alphabet, and it is spoken only in Greece.

In a kindergarten TBE class in one of these districts there are 11 students, but only 7 are from Greek-speaking families. The other four are there because the program has a reputation for being accelerated—they do not know any Greek at all. Not surprisingly, given the presence of students from a non-Greek background, these students are taught almost entirely in English with about 45 minutes of Greek instruction each day, which consists of the alphabet and simple vocabulary. Even the students from Greek-speaking families are not fluent in Greek, so the students are on more even ground than one might expect in such a classroom.

While the kindergarten Greek TBE program is in a self-contained classroom, the students in grades 1 through 6 in the same school are pulled out of monolingual English classrooms for Greek instruction as educational enrichment. The Greek TBE teacher for these grades has not heard of the theory behind transitional bilingual education. She subscribes to a different theory—that students are better off knowing more than one language.

RUSSIAN

The Russian LEP population is also small in Massachusetts—about 1,300 students in 31 TBE districts. Ten of these districts have more than 20 Russian LEP students, but only three have more than 130. Among these students are immigrants from the former Soviet Union who do not actually speak Russian, but speak other languages, such as Ukrainian.

The Russian language does not use the Roman alphabet. Russian TBE programs are pullout programs in which a Russian TBE teacher assists students with English and occasionally translates. Sometimes, a little Russian may be taught to students who want to learn the language. In one pullout program, every Russian-speaking LEP student is sent to the Russian TBE teacher for testing, evaluation, and help in English. As they are taught in all-English classrooms, her role is to help them become fluent in English. She believes she could be fired if the state department of education learned she was not teaching them in their native language. She says she could never justify in her own mind the amount of time Russian language instruction would take away from their English instruction. When asked why she thinks the state requires native tongue instruction, she replies that the state does not realize that Russian speakers do not need such a "crutch. They can handle English language instruction."

One ESL teacher teaches English to classes of LEP students from different language groups, including Russian. She does not believe her inability to speak Russian is any detriment to her Russian-speaking students; she is able to teach them English without translating at all.

In another school, the Russian TBE teacher offers Russian-speaking students help in various subjects, but an ESL teacher assists them with English. The Russian TBE teacher organizes a variety of activities that include the entire school to give all the students a greater appreciation of Russian culture. The Russian TBE program has a dual purpose—academic help for LEP students and support of a multicultural curriculum.

Chinese

While Chinese is routinely listed as a language group, there is no spoken Chinese language per se. The official language of China is Mandarin, one of many spoken dialects. Yet the state department of education lists "Chinese" as a language in its transitional bilingual education reports. According to the state, there are more than 3,000 LEP "Chinese" speakers in 45 TBE districts. Twenty-two districts have more than 20 students, and three have more than 130. (The state also lists the "Canton dialect" as having 12 speakers.)

Written Chinese, which is the same for all dialects, is ideographic, does not use a phonetic alphabet, is difficult to learn, and bears no resemblance to English. The effort required to teach Cantonese- or Mandarin- or Toisanese-speaking children to read in Chinese would be extraordinary and the skills transferable to English very limited—if one had enough students who spoke the same dialect to fill a classroom and a certified teacher to teach them.

In a first grade "Chinese" TBE class, there are 24 Chinese students; 22 speak Cantonese and 2 Mandarin. The teacher is fluent in Cantonese but not Mandarin. She teaches in English and responds, even to questions asked in Cantonese, in English. She does not believe learning to read and write in the native language would facilitate learning in English. She sees the purpose of the Chinese TBE program as maintaining the culture of the Chinese community. She reports that the parents of her students want their children to learn English and actually discourage them from learning their native language, a fact the teacher finds sad, but she would not consider including native tongue instruction in the regular school day.

Second and third grade classes observed are also taught entirely in English; some teachers do hang simple Chinese characters on the wall and teach the students the characters. But even native speakers teach subject matter in English and use the native language only to help recent immigrants or as a last resort. Some teachers expressed regret that parents do not support and children do not have any opportunity for learning to read and write in Chinese.

THE 1993 EOE SURVEY OF TBE DISTRICTS

Thirty-seven, or 72.5 percent, of the 51 TBE districts responded to the 1992-93 Executive Office of Education survey of TBE school districts.[11] Very few school districts admitted having any kind of program other than TBE, defined in the survey as

> a general, self-contained program model where students receive content area instruction in their native language while they are introduced to English. More and more English is gradually added to their curriculum as the students acquire

> the language. The student in a TBE program is mainstreamed for physical education, art, and music (p.1).

Several said they had TBE and for the smaller language groups some form of tutoring. Only two school districts claimed to have the integrative model of bilingual education, defined in the survey as follows:

> Integrated Bilingual Education connects existing bilingual and mainstream classes and teachers, preserving bilingual education for students in the TBE program. Mix groups for some content area instruction. At other times TBE students are grouped by themselves for instruction in a content area in a language other than English, or for concentrated ESL. Mainstream students take some courses that are taught bilingually (p.1).

Based on our observations, neither of the two districts that said they had an integrated bilingual education program actually had one since neither had a self-contained bilingual classroom. Both school districts simply enrolled LEP students in a regular classroom and provided an ESL and/or bilingual teacher on a pullout basis. Other school districts admitted to providing only tutoring for some language groups even though there were 20 or more students. The law requires that TBE be full-time, and not a pullout program, and include instruction in the reading and writing of the child's native language and the history and culture of their native country, when there are 20 or more LEP students of a single language group in the district. All the districts claimed to be providing TBE at least for the Spanish speakers, and the majority claimed to be providing TBE for the other language groups whenever they were greater than 20.

Based on our observations, native tongue instruction is likely only if all the following conditions are met: 1) LEP students number at least 10 per grade at the elementary level (with two grades being combined to form one classroom of at least 20) or 20 per grade at the secondary level; 2) school staff believe that the students comprising a particular language group do not possess the academic skills necessary for success in an all-English, regular education environment; 3) the teacher is fluent in the native language of all the students in a single class; 4) the native language is the official language of one or more large countries or areas; 5) the language uses a Roman alphabet, and there are written materials applicable to a U.S. curriculum, including textbooks in various subjects and storybooks. Figure 4-8 graphically illustrates these conditions. If none of these conditions are met, the program is likely to be one in which the students are taught completely in English or mostly in English with the occasional use of the native tongue for *assistance,* not instruction. The law, however, does not recognize these pedagogical and social realities, and so school districts in Massachusetts are forced to obfuscate when the state comes calling. This is evident in the EOE survey responses.

Figure 4-8
Observed Criteria for Placement of LEP Elementary School Students in State-Funded Bilingual Programs

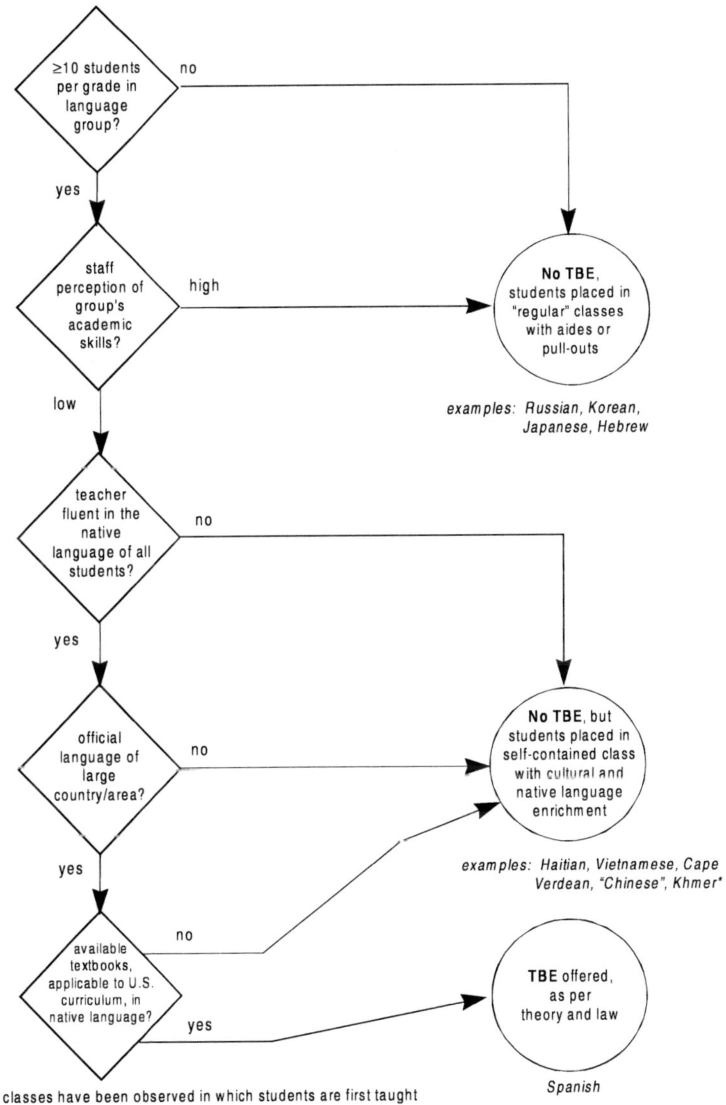

* Khmer classes have been observed in which students are first taught English and then after achieving some proficiency are taught Khmer.

Using the logic suggested by the conditions above, only 22 percent of the TBE school districts are capable of offering TBE to all LEP students who comprise 20 or more of a single language group. Another 32 percent can provide TBE to Spanish-speaking LEP students but not to other language minority groups. For example, a school district with 2,413 Spanish speakers enrolled in TBE programs might actually be offering something close to what the law requires. But this same school district claims also to be providing TBE for 13 Portuguese speakers. Even combining four grades, the maximum allowed by the regulations, means a self-contained classroom of four students on average taught by a bilingual teacher with an average salary of $39,012 for a per-pupil TBE expenditure of $9,753 (excluding all other non-teacher costs), almost twice the state average of $5,234 (which includes all costs).

Thirty percent of the respondents to the Executive Office of Education survey claimed to be offering a Portuguese TBE program at the secondary level. Almost half of those claiming to offer "Portuguese" TBE, however, followed the word with a slash and "Kriolu" or "Cape Verdean" or "CV" indicating that it is Cape Verdeans who are enrolled in the program. It is possible that the other half of respondents claiming to have Portuguese TBE just neglected to add the adjective Cape Verdean since all but three indicated a Cape Verdean LEP high school population. One school district claimed to be offering a Greek TBE program at the secondary level, and one also claimed to be offering a Russian TBE program at the secondary level.

Another school district claims to be providing a Spanish TBE program to 165 Spanish speakers. It is not likely, however, that this same school district is providing a similar TBE program for 74 Chinese students (10 per classroom with two grades combined), 46 Korean students (7 per classroom with two grades combined), and 15 Ethiopian students (2 per classroom with two grades combined), as claimed in the survey response. In fact, the "limit" of 10 per grade as a likely predictor of true bilingual education is probably too generous since school officials are loath to combine grades for a full-time self-contained classroom even for the purpose of bilingual education. They would much prefer to put LEP children in a regular classroom consisting of only one grade and pull the students out for individualized instruction as needed. Indeed, in 15 years of observing hundreds of (at least nominally) bilingual education classrooms, we have observed only a handful of self-contained classrooms with more than one grade and only once encountered three grades combined. We have *never* encountered, in Massachusetts or elsewhere, four grades combined in one full-time self-contained classroom, the limit set by the state department of education.

CONCLUSION

The actual implementation of transitional bilingual education is thus far afield from the theory, from the law, and from the regulations. It is possible that because there was an observer in their classroom and the law requires native tongue instruction the Spanish TBE teachers taught more in Spanish than they would have ordinarily. Indeed, given how often teachers apologized to me when they had to teach in English while I was there, it appears that the bias is to want to teach in Spanish for the benefit of an observer. However, it also appears that this bias is fairly small since I saw many lessons in English accompanied by the explanation that this was the English lesson period and they did not want to deviate from the day's lesson plan. In addition, the non-Spanish TBE teachers taught completely in English and readily admitted they always did so despite the fact that they were violating the law. Therefore, while there was probably a tendency to teach more in Spanish than might ordinarily occur, we do not believe it was enough to change our conclusions—only Spanish speakers receive native tongue instruction, and even they do not always receive it to the extent that the law and the theory demand.

A program with this much disparity between theory, law, and actual practice must be questioned. We are of the opinion that the theory and the law are unrealistic given real world fiscal and pedagogical constraints and that state officials understand this and as a result tolerate considerable, albeit unacknowledged, deviation from the law. State officials probably understand that school districts operate in the real world where there are not enough bilingual teachers. Even if there were enough teachers, the taxpayers, in any case, would be unwilling to fund the writing and publication of textbooks in little-spoken dialects for classrooms of a few students. Even if they were willing, many teachers dispute the utility of teaching children to read and write in languages that no one writes in or that bear no resemblance to English.

Appendix 4-1
Number of LEP Students in Each State by Program Enrollment 1991–1992

State	Bilingual	ESL	Un-known	Total	% LEP
Alabama	350	124	0	474	0.1
Alaska	12,056	0	0	12,056	9.8
Arizona	17,146	38,085	3,396	58,627	8.7
Arkansas	na	na	na	na	0.0
California	659,822	161,689	0	821,511	15.8
Colorado	1,155	9,401	6,762	17,318	2.8
Connecticut	12,848	2,368	0	15,216	3.1
Delaware	na	na	907	907	0.9
Dist. of Col.	209	3,252	0	3,461	4.3
Florida	3,809	720	79,296	83,825	4.2
Georgia	0	6,737	0	6,737	0.6
Hawaii	10,335	0	0	10,355	5.8
Idaho	336	3,911	0	4,247	1.8
Illinois	61,335	20,514	0	81,849	4.4
Indiana	915	715	346	1,976	0.2
Iowa	942	3,238	na	4,180	0.8
Kansas	417	2,278	3,269	5,964	1.3
Kentucky	780	na	486	1,266	0.2
Louisiana	648	3,646	2,564	6,858	0.9
Maine	299	870	na	1,169	0.5
Maryland	406	6,526	5,169	12,101	1.6
Mass.	38,043	0	0	38,043	4.4
Michigan	18,475	0	0	18,475	1.2
Minnesota	4,235	188	10,613	15,036	1.9
Mississippi	626	865	na	1,491	0.3
Missouri	425	185	na	610	0.1
Montana	1,901	94	1,850	3,845	2.4
Nebraska	202	1,063	na	1,265	0.4
Nevada	226	3,157	6,301	9,684	4.3

Appendix 4-1 (cont'd.)
Number of LEP Students in Each State by Program Enrollment 1991–1992

State	Bilingual	ESL	Un-known	Total	% LEP
New Hamp.	39	123	429	591	0.3
New Jersey	2,649	na	42,555	45,204	4.0
New Mexico	74,421	58	na	74,479	23.6
New York	19,468	na	129,238	148,706	5.5
N. Carolina	253	541	2,250	3,044	0.3
North Dakota	1,384	482	na	1,866	1.6
Ohio	3,018	2,815	3,219	9,052	0.5
Oklahoma	1,480	1,595	11,758	14,833	2.5
Oregon	2,305	750	6,402	9,457	1.9
Pennsyl.	na	na	na	na	0.0
Rhode Island	1,493	6,410	na	7,903	5.5
S. Carolina	133	681	295	1,109	0.2
S. Dakota	1,332	na	1,556	2,888	2.1
Tennessee	na	na	2,519	2,519	0.3
Texas	152,553	129,366	10	281,929	8.0
Utah	85	na	2,499	2,584	0.6
Vermont	na	180	115	295	0.3
Virginia	na	na	na	na	0.0
Washington	7,387	na	26,517	33,904	3.8
West Virginia	na	na	na	na	0.0
Wisconsin	10,680	249	2,751	13,680	1.6
Wyoming	122	92	536	750	0.7
TOTAL	1,126,393	412,844	353,608	1,892,845	4.4
AVERAGE					2.7

Source: American Legislative Exchange Council (ALEC), *Report Card on American Education 1994: A State-by-State Analysis*, Washington, D.C., 1994.

Appendix 4-2
51 Massachusetts TBE Districts

Amherst
Amherst-Pelham
Attleboro
Barnstable
Boston
Brockton
Brookline
Cambridge
Chelsea
Chicopee
Clinton
Fall River
Fitchburg
Framingham
Haverhill
Holyoke
Hudson
Lawrence
Lawrence Voc. T.
Leominster
Lexington
Lowell
Lowell Voc. T.
Ludlow
Lynn
Malden
Marlborough
Medford
Methuen
Milford
New Bedford
New Bedford Voc. T.
Newton
Northampton
Peabody
Quincy
Randolph
Revere
Salem
Scituate
Somerville
Southbridge
Springfield
S. Middlesex Voc. T.
Stoughton
Taunton
Waltham
Watertown
Westfield
West Springfield
Worcester

Source: Massachusetts Department of Education, *Transitional Bilingual Education Report, Year Ending June 30, 1993*, table 1; Massachusetts Department of Education, Office of Planning, Research and Evaluation, Individual School Report, October 1, 1992, table 3.

Appendix 4-3
Language Minority Groups In Massachusetts
1992–93

	Language Minority	Enrollment in TBE	LEP Total
Afrikaans	9	0	3
Albanian	13	0	8
Amharic	29	13	18
Arabic	532	4	221
Armenian	137	21	70
Bahasa/ Indonesian	2	0	1
Bengali	31	0	17
Bulgarian	5	0	3
Burmese	11	0	0
Canton Dialect	12	0	6
Cape Verdean	3,751	1,530	2,230
Chichewa	1	0	0
Chinese	5,595	1,733	3,112
Creole (Haitian)	4,774	2,019	2,960
Czech	22	0	7
Danish	9	0	6
Dutch	11	0	6
Farsi	60	0	24
Finnish	4	0	3
Flemish	1	0	1
French	352	0	25
French Patois	26	0	2
Fr./African Patois	24	0	18
Frisian	3	0	0
Galla	3	0	0
German	52	0	19
Greek	1,005	176	375
Guarani	3	0	3
Gujarati	229	58	114
Hakka Dialect	1	0	1
Hebrew	415	95	177
Hindi	123	0	37

Appendix 4-3 (cont'd)
Language Minority Groups In Massachusetts
1992–93

	Language Minority	Enrollment in TBE	LEP Total
Hmong	154	0	93
Hungarian	23	0	7
Ibo	8	0	4
Icelandic	2	0	0
Indian	44	0	8
Indo-European	1	0	0
Italian	750	0	338
Jamaican Creole	4	0	0
Japanese	340	162	227
Javanese	1	0	0
Khmer	5,726	2,333	2,956
Kinyarwandu	2	0	1
Korean	440	63	241
Krio	8	0	8
Lao	958	253	438
Latvian	3	0	3
Lithuanian	3	0	1
Luganda	5	0	1
Macedonian	1	0	1
Malay	13	0	4
Mandarin/ Chinese	13	0	13
Nepali	3	0	2
Newari	1	0	0
Norwegian	2	0	2
Persian	18	0	2
Pilipino	37	0	14
Polish	372	82	193
Portuguese	11,177	2,240	3,134
Romanian	11	0	8
Russian	2,008	951	1,345
Samoan	1	0	1
Serbo Croatian	14	0	4

Appendix 4-3 (cont'd)
Language Minority Groups In Massachusetts
1992–93

	Language Minority	Enrollment in TBE	LEP Total
Siswati	1	0	0
Slovak	8	0	3
Somali	6	0	6
Spanish	56,342	24,110	29,868
Swahili	4	0	2
Swedish	7	0	0
Taiwan	4	0	1
Tamil	11	0	10
Thai	37	1	17
Tibetan	2	0	0
Tigre	1	0	1
Turkish	30	1	10
Urdu	51	0	31
Vietnamese	5,629	1,938	3,541
Yiddish	1	0	1
Other	188	11	129
TOTAL	62,322	37,794	52,136

Source: Massachusetts Department of Education, *Transitional Bilingual Education Report, Year Ending June 30, 1993*, table 2.

CHAPTER FIVE

SELECTING AND EXITING STUDENTS IN BILINGUAL EDUCATION PROGRAMS

There is surprisingly little academic discussion in the bilingual education literature concerning the difficulty of correctly identifying students who do not speak English in order to determine who should enter and exit from the programs. In general, analyses of the procedures for identifying and exiting students have been limited to theoretical discussions of the notion that language consists of discrete, separable structures,[1] the adequacy of tests for demonstrating the learner's true level of proficiency in the new language,[2] and the tests' cultural bias,[3] normalization or standardization procedures,[4] and technical validity.[5] If there is any criticism, it is generally that the tests do not identify *enough* students because they do not assess advanced "academic" skills.[6] Very few analysts have come to the conclusion that the tests ought to be abandoned or that they are overinclusive—that is, identifying and retaining too many, rather than too few students. Our previous writings on this subject are the exception to the rule.[7]

Most analyses of bilingual education, however, are silent on the issue of whether any of the procedures used to select and exit students are valid. The 1994 report of the Massachusetts Bilingual Education Commission, *Striving for Success: The Education of Bilingual Pupils,* for example, discusses the diversity of the population of LEP children, how long they are in TBE, the shortage of bilingual certified teachers and the requirements for certification, the involvement of parents, the effectiveness of the programs, the place of the program in the school, and the funding of TBE, but not the problem of defining limited english proficiency in order to identify children for inclusion in these programs correctly. Like most analyses, this report appears to assume that identification is done correctly and that the only issue of controversy is how long children stay in bilingual education programs.

The laws have also largely ignored the issue. The 1968 Bilingual Education Act (Title VII of the Elementary and Secondary Education Act) defined the target group for bilingual education as those children who are educationally disadvantaged because of their inability to speak English. In 1978 it was further clarified that the purpose of the act was "instruction...in and study of *English* and, to the extent necessary, *to allow a child to achieve competence in the English language,* the native language of the children of limited English proficiency...[emphasis added]."[8] No specific criteria were offered for defining "inability to speak English" or "competence in the English language." The 1968 law defined LEP as follows:

> (A) individuals who were not born in the United States or whose native language is a language other than English; (B) individuals who come from environments where a language other than English is dominant, as further defined by the Secretary by regulation; and (C) individuals who are American Indian and Alaskan Natives who come from environments where a language other than English has a significant impact on the level of English language proficiency.

The 1994 Title VII[9] amendments in the Improving America's Schools Act (formerly the Elementary and Secondary Education Act) emphasize for the first time the development of the cognitive abilities of LEP children and the development of the native language as a goal of the legislation:

> The purpose of this part is to educate limited English proficient children and youth to meet the same rigorous standards for academic performance expected of all children and youth, including meeting challenging State content standards and challenging State student performance standards in academic areas by—(1) developing systemic improvement and reform of educational programs serving limited English proficient students through the development and implementation of exemplary bilingual education programs and special alternative instruction programs; (2) developing *bilingual skills* and multicultural understanding; (3) developing the *English* of such children and youth and, to the extent possible, the native language skills of such children and youth.[10]

The same act defined

> the terms "limited English proficiency" and "limited English proficient", when used with reference to an individual, [to] mean an individual—(A) who—(i) was not born in the United States or whose native language is a language other than English and comes from an environment where a language other than English is dominant; or (ii) is a Native American or Alaska Native who is a resident of the outlying areas and comes from an environment where a language other than English has had a significant impact on such individual's level of English language proficiency; or (iii) is a migratory and whose native language is other than English and comes from an environment where a language other than English is dominant; and (B) who has sufficient difficulty speaking, reading, writing, or understanding the English language and whose difficulties may deny such individual the opportunity to learn successfully in classrooms where the language of instruction is English or to participate fully in our society.[11]

The general presumption of the law is that this is a straightforward process.

The 1971 Massachusetts Transitional Bilingual Education Act, Chapter 71A, was similarly vague on the issue of defining limited English proficiency for entry into TBE education programs, referring to the target of transitional bilingual education programs as students of "limited English-speaking ability." The law does discuss briefly the exiting of students from bilingual education programs:

> ...Every school-age child of limited English-speaking ability...shall be enrolled and participate in the program of transitional bilingual education...for a period of three years or until such time as the student achieves a level of English language skills which will enable the student to perform successfully in classes in which instruction is given only in English, whichever shall first occur.
>
> An examination in the oral comprehension, speaking, reading and writing of English, as prescribed by the department, shall be administered annually to all children of limited English-speaking ability enrolled and participating in a program in transitional bilingual education. No school committee shall transfer a child of limited English-speaking ability out of a program in transitional bilingual education prior to the student's third year of enrollment therein unless the parents of the child approve the transfer in writing, and unless the child has received a score on said examination which, in the determination of the department, reflects a level of English language skills appropriate to his or her grade level.[12]

Clearly, the intent of both the federal and Massachusetts law is that the recipients of bilingual education be children who speak little or no English and are in need of a special language program in order to acquire enough English to allow them to participate successfully in the regular classroom. The theory of bilingual education also assumes this since the only children who could possibly benefit from being taught in their native language are those who know that language better than they know English. Thus, it is important that it be accurately determined whether a child knows his or her native language better than English.

State Policies

From 1964 to 1975, the states were guided by Title VI of the 1964 Civil Rights Act, which forbade discrimination by local education agencies receiving federal funds and was enforced by the Office for Civil Rights (OCR). After 1975, the states were obliged to follow the *Lau* guidelines developed by OCR in 1975 to determine if school districts were in compliance with the Supreme Court decision *Lau v. Nichols* (414 U.S. 563, 1974). To identify students in need of bilingual education, the *Lau* guidelines first required that the student's "primary language" be identified. A student was considered to have a primary language other than English if any of three conditions held: 1) the first language the student spoke was not English, 2) the language most often spoken in the student's home was not English, or 3) the language most often spoken by the student was other than English. With all these criteria, however, a child fully proficient in English could be classified as having a primary language other than English.

In 1991, the Council of Chief State School Officers compiled data on state practices regarding the assessment of LEP students.[13] Twenty-eight out of 51 states, including Massachusetts, have state laws or regulations that determine how students are identified as LEP. These 28 and 10 others provide local school districts with procedures for the identification of LEP students. All but Arkansas collect data about LEP students.

States generally use one or more of six methods to identify LEP students needing services. In general, school districts have a lot of flexibility in choosing methods for identifying LEP students. Only 22 states—Massachusetts included—have mandated one or more methods to be used in this process. Among the most frequently used methods is the *home language survey*, a short form administered in writing or through interviews by school systems to determine the home language environment. Massachusetts is one of 18 states that mandate the home language survey as the first step in the identification process. The information collected in the home language survey varies from state to state. The questions deal with the language primarily used at home, first acquired, used most frequently, spoken to parents, spoken to siblings, and spoken to friends. Fifteen states either do not collect this information or, as is the case with Massachusetts, allow school districts to determine their own home language survey questions.

Another procedure required or recommended by the states is the collection of *registration and enrollment information* from all incoming students. This usually includes information similar to that collected in the home language survey, such as the use of language(s) other than English, in addition to other demographic and/or academic background information. Identification through *observation* is often done by a teacher or aide who has heard a student using a language other than English. *Interviews* for identification may include an oral assessment of a student through conversation, a conversation with parents, or both. Since *tests* are believed to be more objective in evaluating a student's ability, they are mandated in 13 states and recommended in 22 others for identifying LEP students. *Referrals* are often made by teachers, counselors, parents, administrators, or community organizations for further assessment, usually at some central office.

Massachusetts has three approved tests, the Language Assessment Scales (LAS), the IDEA Oral Language Proficiency Test (IPT), and the Bilingual Syntax Measure (BSM).[14] However, it is left up to the school districts to decide 1) whether they even use the tests to determine eligibility for a program, and 2) what cut-off point they use.

Determining eligibility for language assistance programs is only half the problem. Once students are enrolled in a program, some procedure has to be created to determine when they are ready to exit. There are a number of techniques used to assess whether a child is ready to be mainstreamed, including observation, interview, content area test, language proficiency test, parent consent, and committee decision. One-third of the states require a language proficiency test before a child can be mainstreamed. Altogether about one-third of the states require one of these methods to determine eligibility for exit.[15]

Massachusetts law requires only that students not be exited prior to the student's third year of enrollment "or until such time as the student achieves a level of English language skills which will enable the student to perform successfully in classes in which instruction is given only in English, whichever shall first occur."[16] No specific procedure is mandated to determine this in Massachusetts except that the exit decision must be by committee. Although tests are not required, if they are used they must be among those approved for annual testing of TBE students.

Twelve states require that districts use state-approved tests, and 10 require a specific cut-off that is around the 35th to 40th percentile for standardized achievement tests and the 50th to 85th percentile for English language proficiency tests. Massachusetts requires neither an exit test nor a cut-off point that automatically classifies a student as eligible to be mainstreamed.[17]

The procedures mandated by the states demonstrate four things. First, they show a profound faith in the ability of standardized tests to identify students in need of bilingual instruction, although this is less true in Massachusetts than in other states. Second, they evidence a strong belief in the value of bilingual education. Children in grade two or below could be placed in bilingual education for two or three years solely on the basis of the home language survey, and they cannot be exited without demonstrating proficiency in English, usually by means of a standardized test, and in many states, they must score above a required cut-off. Third, there is no agreement among states as to the criteria by which students are to be selected and exited from bilingual education programs. Finally, there is little awareness that the criteria for entry and exit are in fact arbitrary. As we shall see, this only reflects the lack of academic agreement on this issue.

HOW SCHOOL DISTRICTS IDENTIFY STUDENTS

Title VII of the Improving America's Schools Act requires no specific assessment procedures for identifying LEP students in school districts receiving federal funds. In their grant applications, districts simply have to present data on the number of children of limited English proficiency in the school or school district to be served and their characteristics, such as language spoken, dropout rates, proficiency in English and the native language, academic standing in relation to their English-proficient peers, and where applicable, when they immigrated.

We could find only three studies on how school districts actually identify students for participation in bilingual programs. Mace-Matluck (1982) characterized selection procedures as including a home language survey, an oral language proficiency test, and some use of standardized English reading and writing tests, usually from grade 2 up.[18] Cardoza (1984) found that 90 percent of the school districts surveyed used an English oral proficiency test, 72 percent measured English reading, 56 percent measured English writing skills, and 64 percent assessed student native language skills.[19]

The most detailed data seem to be in Young et al. (1984).[20] This study examined a nationally representative sample of 229 school districts serving LM-LEP (language minority/limited English proficiency) students and found that the judgment of teachers and staff appears to play a major role in actual school selection procedures. About two-thirds of all LM-LEP students were screened by procedures that included staff judgment. In addition, both Mace-Matluck and Cardoza found widespread use of teacher recommendations in the procedures for exiting the bilingual program.

Several school districts—Amherst, Boston, Brookline, and Fitchburg—attached copies of their assessment procedures to their completed Executive Office of Education questionnaires. The Boston home language survey is typical of those used in the other districts. It asks parents to fill in basic demographic data such as their country of birth and highest grade completed and to check the appropriate box indicating which of 19 languages they understand best. Finally, parents are asked to respond to the following questions about the home environment:

1. What language(s) are spoken and/or understood by people living in your home?
2. What was the first language your child spoke?
3. What language does your child use when speaking with you?
4. What language does your child use when speaking with brothers and sisters?
5. What language does your child use when speaking with other family members?
6. What language does your child use when speaking with friends in the neighborhood?

If a parent answers any one of these questions with a language other than English, the child is considered potentially LEP and referred for testing to the Translation and Assessment Center (TAC) at 26 Court Street. The TAC staff will recommend a TBE program or a regular mainstream program for the child depending on the results on the IPT and the Cloze test, two English language proficiency tests—the former oral, the latter reading. Students are also tested in their native language. There is no specific score that automatically assigns a child to a bilingual program or to any specific program. Students who are classified as fluent in English on the basis of the English proficiency tests do not have to take a standardized achievement test as they would in many school districts throughout the United States. The test scores are forwarded by the TAC to the school, where it becomes part of the information used to assign students to classrooms.

The Fitchburg home language survey consists of six questions very similar to those used in Boston. A response to any of the questions indicating a non-English language will trigger the next step—oral proficiency tests in English and the native tongue. In the case of low incidence populations, the testing will be done only in English. Unlike Boston, however, the Fitchburg school district administers reading and writing tests (the LAS/R and the LAS/W) if the student shows near fluent oral English proficiency. An informal interview is conducted with the parent and the student to assess educational history and any special problems relevant to school placement. The tester then confers with a school team to ensure the proper placement.

The Brookline home language survey consists of five questions: 1) In what language do you speak to your child at home? 2) In what language does your child speak to you? 3) In what language does your child respond to other adults living at home? 4) What language did your child first learn? and 5) What language does your child use with peers or siblings at home? If two or more responses are a language other than English, students are referred for language assessment. The assessment consists of three parts: 1) an oral interview for gathering information and assessing listening and speaking skills, 2) a reading assessment, and 3) a writing assessment. The reading assessment is a reading readiness interview for grades K and 1 and the Cloze test for grades 2 through 12. The writing assessment is administered to grades 2 through 12. Students are asked to write a paragraph about something that interests them. The information from all these different sources is then summarized on a student language assessment form, and a decision is made by the school district assessment team as to the proper placement for the child.

The Amherst (Elementary) School District follows the same basic model. First, a home language survey is administered with similar questions, although this survey asks for evidence of language switching in communication with parents and siblings and asks the parents to assess the language their child understands best at this time. A student who is identified as having a home language other than English is then referred for testing in the areas of listening, speaking, reading, and writing at an age, grade, and language appropriate level. Listening and speaking are assessed by the BSM and reading by a number of different measures depending on the age of the child.[21] Writing is assessed by the Modern American English Diagnostic Test and the LAS. In addition, there is a whole battery of tests in Chinese (including listening and speaking—both an impossibility), Khmer, and Spanish. Upon completion of testing in English, and where possible the native language, the child's classroom teacher is consulted for help in determining a recommendation for the student's academic program.

The selection procedures actually used by school districts thus seem to be reducible to three steps: 1) a home language survey is conducted to identify the potential pool of LEP students, 2) the students identified in the home language survey are tested on some measure of academic performance and classified accordingly, and 3) the decision is tempered by staff judgment, either the child's classroom teacher or a team of professionals employed by the school district.

The decision to exit a student from bilingual education or special language assistance involves procedures similar to those used to determine eligibility. Obviously, the home language survey is eliminated since that information was obtained on entry. In Massachusetts, students in TBE cannot be exited from the program prior to the third year unless they have achieved exit scores on an examination in the oral comprehension, speaking, reading, and writing of English, which in the determination of the state department of education reflect a level of English language skills appropriate to their grade level. As discussed above, no minimum score is specified by the standard, and districts are encouraged to use a holistic approach.

This occurs in the four districts mentioned above—Amherst, Boston, Brookline, and Fitchburg—in very similar ways. Annual testing is conducted using the state-approved tests, and a committee of school professionals, including the student's classroom teachers, reviews the test results and decides whether the student can be partially or wholly mainstreamed. The approach in all four school districts is holistic, including not only standardized test scores but teacher evaluations and other informal assessment practices, as recommended by the state department of education.

The state of Massachusetts keeps statistics, summarized in *Striving for Success,* on how long students are in bilingual education in each of the TBE districts.[22] This report shows that only 23 percent of the original TBE population are still enrolled in a TBE program by the fourth year, and only 16 percent are still enrolled by the fifth year. These data, however, cannot be wholly trusted as a student who moves from one school district to another and enrolls in TBE is often counted as a new TBE student in the second district even though he or she may have been in TBE in the first. There is some suspicion that this happens when students move from one school to another within the same district as well. Thus, it is not known to what extent the reliance on tests tends to keep TBE students in Massachusetts from being mainstreamed. Nor is it clear to what extent staff judgment enables or prevents the mainstreaming of students.

Except for the role of staff judgment, the procedures used in Massachusetts and in other states largely correspond to what the bilingual education advocates and plaintiffs in bilingual education litigation have demanded. The question we turn to now is whether these procedures are valid.

The Social Science Evidence on Assessment Procedures

Home Language Surveys

Home language surveys, the first step in the assessment process for most states, frequently ask if *someone* in the home, not just the target child, speaks a language other than English. As there are large intergenerational differences in language use among immigrant groups, the fact that a child's parents or grandparents speak Spanish is no indication of what language the child speaks.

California's home language survey is one of the more complex and, on the face of it, seems to correct this problem. Until recently it included four questions:

1. Which language did your son or daughter learn when he or she first began to talk?

2. What language does your son or daughter most frequently use at home?

3. What language do you use most frequently to speak to your son or daughter?

4. Name the languages in the order most often spoken by the adults at home.

While this survey appears to be more sensitive than most, including those used in Massachusetts, because it asks about the *frequency* of language use, the way in which the results are interpreted makes it as overinclusive as the simpler surveys. Until recently, a response other than English to *any* of the four questions classified the student as having a home language other than English. This included a response of "English and another language" to any of the four questions. Recently the last question was dropped as a means of classification. Nevertheless, if a parent answered English to the first two questions and English and Vietnamese to the third, the child would be classified as having Vietnamese as his or her home language and be identified as potentially in need of instruction in a language he or she does not speak in order to improve his or her English. This type of error is equally possible in Boston and other school districts in Massachusetts. If it occurs, the rest of the procedures commonly used will not always correct the mistake.

STANDARDIZED ACHIEVEMENT TESTS

The reliance on standardized achievement tests and the assumption that they are a superior means of identifying students who need bilingual education is evident in the court decisions over the last decade.[23] The *Keyes* procedures (*Keyes v. School District No. 1*, 576 F. Supp. 1503, 1983), and others like them, place an elementary student from a non-English home language background into the bilingual program and keep him there if he scores below the 30th percentile on a standardized achievement test (for example, the CTBS). As the California Supreme Court noted, however, in *Jimenez v. Honig* (188 Cal. App. 3d 1034, 233 Cal. Rptr. 817, 1987), standardized tests are designed so that 30 percent of the students will score at or below the

30th percentile. Therefore, some unknown percentage of the English-speaking students identified by the home language survey as potentially LEP could be misclassified as in need of bilingual education by the standardized tests. If these same tests are used to determine whether a student is able to exit a bilingual program, some unknown percentage will never get out. Because language minority students come from socioeconomically disadvantaged backgrounds, more than 30 percent will score below the 30th percentile because disadvantaged students score lower on standardized tests than the general population on which these tests were normed.[24]

Keith Baker participated in extensive discussions with the OCR staff during the development of the proposed 1980 *Lau* regulations. When questioned about the justification for the percentile cutoffs used, the OCR staff responded that they had picked a score that people agreed identified a student who was not doing well in school. While that may very well be true, such a score does not tell us that this student needs special language instruction because it cannot differentiate among the several possible causes of a low score. Indeed, it is unlikely that any cutoff score will be valid for this purpose.[25]

A final problem with using standardized tests is that a single test in one language—English—is not enough information by which to determine if a student no longer needs extra help. Consider the following thought experiment. Imagine a Vietnamese refugee child, 10 years old, who enrolls in a school where the 30th percentile is the cutoff score for bilingual education. She is tested and found to score at the 35th percentile. No special help will be provided for her. Somehow, her family managed to bring along her school records from Vietnam, and they show that, when tested in Vietnamese, she performed at the 85th percentile. Thus, this is a student who might be able to benefit from special help because she has a lot of English to learn before she can realize her potential in the regular English-speaking classroom.

Now imagine another Vietnamese refugee in a similar situation who tests at the 20th percentile in English. He is put into the bilingual program. His Vietnamese test records, however, show he also performed at the 20th percentile in that language. This student may have learned English to the full level of his potential and may not benefit from special help. Furthermore, if the exit criterion is the 35th percentile, a common standard, this student could be in transitional bilingual education his entire school career.

We see in these two hypothetical situations that the wrong decision is made in both cases by the reliance on standardized test scores. Rather than correcting the misclassification errors made by the home language survey, the standardized tests add misclassification errors of their own.

LANGUAGE PROFICIENCY TESTS

Virtually all selection methods use language proficiency tests, alone or in conjunction with standardized tests. Rather than solving the problem, these procedures merely exchange one inappropriately used test for another. Following the passage of state legislation requiring language competency tests, both California and Texas, which combined have about 55 percent of the language minority population in the United States, assembled blue-ribbon commissions to identify and recommend satisfactory language competency tests for use in their respective states. Both commissions concluded there were *no* psychometrically acceptable language competency tests in existence.[26] Other analyses of language proficiency tests, including one conducted by the Massachusetts Bureau of TBE, have confirmed their lack of reliability and validity.[27] Nevertheless, Massachusetts, like California, Texas, and other states, disseminated a list of approved tests to school districts. Massachusetts school districts were free to choose whatever test they wanted to use until 1990, when Elizabeth Twomey, Associate Commissioner of School Programs, and Gilman Hebert, Director of the then Bureau of Equity and Language Services, sent out a letter to superintendents in Massachusetts advising them of the appropriate tests. The letter conveys to the school districts a misleading picture of the validity and reliability of these tests:

> The appropriate monitoring of a student's educational progress as well as documentation of the benefit of the Transitional Bilingual Program as a whole has suffered from the lack of a uniform instrument. Twelve reading and writing evaluation instruments were thoroughly reviewed and evaluated on the basis of carefully selected multiple criteria, which included reliability, validity, and norming to language minority students. The advisory committee is unanimous in its judgment that the Language Assessment Scales, Reading/Writing is preferable to all of the others.[28]

Clearly decisions are made about enrolling the majority of the language minority students in this country in bilingual education on the basis of tests that are known to be unreliable or invalid, but whose use is required.

As with standardized achievement tests, one of the most important problems with oral language proficiency tests is that they cannot differentiate students who will do well in school from those who will do poorly.[29] If a test cannot identify those students who will have trouble in school because they lack English language proficiency, assigning students to programs based on the results of such tests is clearly unsound educational practice.

The language proficiency tests share another problem with standardized achievement tests—arbitrary cut-off scores. Lan-guage proficiency is a continuum ranging from no proficiency to full proficiency. Where along this continuum does a student need special language help?

The National Institute of Education (NIE) analyzed the field of relative language assessment for the U.S. Department of Edu-cation and found no agreement as to what language proficiency is. The report cites Spolsky (1978):

> While it may be true that the layman's idea of learning a language is learning words, his criterion for knowing a language is usually expressed quite differently. When he judges his own or anyone else's control of a language, he is more likely to make a functional statement: "I know enough French to read a newspaper," "He can't speak enough English to ask the time of day." Such statements refer to language use and not to grammar or phonology (or vocabulary). The question then arises, how does one go about deciding when someone knows "enough" to carry out a specified function?...[30]

The report also found general agreement that language proficiency tests are unreliable and invalid.

> ...In addition to such problems as low reliability and questionable validity and variation in theoretical underpinnings, differences in quality and quantity of items selected, and the plain fact of the incredible complexity of language, there are serious practical problems associated with assessing language proficiency on the basis of these instruments. Recent empirical studies indicate that the placement of children varies (often significantly) depending on which test is used.[31]

More recently, Irujo, Kramsch, Dube, and Yedlin (1986) surveyed the issue of language proficiency for the Massachusetts Department of Equal Educational Opportunity.[32] They found more than 20 different definitions and concluded that language proficiency is one of the most poorly defined concepts in the field of language education.

Ulibarri, Spencer, and Rivas (1980, 1981), investigating the comparability of three oral English proficiency tests used in California (the LAS, BSM, and Basic Inventory of Natural Language [BINL]), concluded that language classification is a function of the particular test used, with each test identifying different numbers of eligible students. Studies by Gillmore and Dickerson (1979) and Cervantes (1979, 1982) find similar results.[33]

An analysis of more than 2,000 students in six school districts conducted for the US Department of Education by Pelavin and Associates[34] provides us with the most recent information on the reliability of language proficiency tests. The complete set of procedures utilized in the study include 1) two widely used, commercially developed language proficiency tests, the Language Assessment Battery (LAB) and the Language Assessment Scales (LAS)—the latter one of the state-approved tests for Massachusetts districts; 2) a reading subtest from a commercially developed achievement test, the Comprehensive Test of Basic Skills (CTBS); 3) one language dominance measure, the Spanish version of the Language Assessment Scales; and 4) two innovative language proficiency measures, the Minimum English Competency (MEC) Test and the Shell Game.

The MEC test, a 15-question paper and pencil test, was developed by one of the school districts in the sample. Preliminary assessment by the district suggested that it might be able to discriminate between the need for special language services and the need for remedial education.[35] The Shell Game, developed by Wong-Fillmore and McLaughlin,[36] was not used by any of the six districts in the sample and is not commercially available, but its authors believe it is better than most commercial tests at determining whether a student knows enough English to participate in a regular classroom. The test involves recording and coding a child's ability to handle the various functions of academic English encountered in an interactive instructional activity.

An analysis by Pelavin and Baker of pairwise test agreement among the four English language proficiency measures demonstrates that the classification of students as either LEP or English proficient is dependent on the brand of test that is administered. Table 5-1 shows the percentage of agreement between pairs of language proficiency tests for students in the entry sample of 1,100 students who were new to the school district and were being assessed to see if they were eligible for assignment to a bilingual education program. Table 5-2 shows the percentage of agreement between pairs of language proficiency tests for students in the exit sample of 1,100 students who had received some special language services and were being assessed to see if they were proficient enough in English to be mainstreamed.

Table 5-1
Percent of Agreement Between Pairs of Language Proficiency Tests for Students in the Entry Sample

	LAB	MEC	SHELL
LAS	87%	82%	91%
LAB		81%	85%
MEC			80%

Source: Sol Pelavin and Keith Baker, "Improved Methods of Identifying Who Needs Bilingual Education," paper prepared for the annual meeting of the American Educational Research Association, Washington, D.C., 1987.

For the entry sample in table 5-1, the classification agreement[37] between pairs of tests ranges from 80 to 91 percent, with the highest agreement between the Shell Game and the LAS and the lowest agreement between the Shell and the MEC. Agreement between pairs of tests for the exit sample, in table 5-2, is much lower. Here the range of pairwise agreement is only 58 to 72 percent, with the highest agreement between the LAS and the LAB and the lowest agreement between the MEC and the LAS.

Table 5-2
Percent of Agreement Between Pairs of Language Proficiency Tests for Students in the Exit Sample

	LAB	MEC	SHELL
LAS	72%	58%	69%
LAB		61%	69%
MEC			68%

Source: Sol Pelavin and Keith Baker, "Improved Methods of Identifying Who Needs Bilingual Education," paper prepared for the annual meeting of the American Educational Research Association, Washington, D.C., 1987.

The lower agreement among the tests in the exit sample than among those in the entry sample suggests that the disagreement between tests occurs mainly for those students who spoke some English, a more likely occurrence with exit students than with entry students. To test this hypothesis, Pelavin and Baker selected those students who were classified as English-proficient by at least one of the four tests. As shown in table 5-3, the test agreement among these students was low, from 51 to 69 percent for the combined entry and exit samples. Thus, the classification of students who speak some English is highly dependent on the test being used.

Table 5-3
Percent of Agreement Between Pairs of Language Proficiency Tests or Students Classified as English Proficient by at Least One Test
(Entry and Exit Samples Combined)

	LAB	MEC	SHELL
LAS	66%	51%	69%
LAB		52%	60%
MEC			52%

Source: Sol Pelavin and Keith Baker, "Improved Methods of Identifying Who Needs Bilingual Education," paper prepared for the annual meeting of the American Educational Research Association, Washington, D.C., 1987.

Another commonly used language proficiency test is the IDEA Oral Language Proficiency Test (IPT). It is one of the language proficiency tests approved by the Massachusetts Department of Education and is used by many school districts in the state, including the Boston Public Schools. Research conducted by Ramirez and Ramey (1986) shows the IPT to be quite unreliable. Of 573 kindergarten students classified as Non-English-Speaking, Limited-English-Speaking, or Fluent-English-Speaking in the fall of 1984 in California, 236 had moved up one category, 238 had stayed the same, and 99 had moved *down* one category or more by the spring of 1986. Thus, according to this test 40 percent of the sample had made no progress in English over two years, and 17 percent knew less English than when they began.

Similar results are found with students in higher grades. Of 232 first graders classified in the fall of 1984, 50 percent made no progress over two years, and 13 percent knew less English than when they began according to the IPT. Of 123 third graders classified by the IPT in the fall of 1984, 48 percent seemingly made no progress, and 7 percent knew less English than when they began.[38] This is obviously highly unlikely.

In short, the research evidence indicates that language proficiency tests are unreliable and invalid, and there is a good deal of disagreement between the different types, particularly when the students tested speak some English. Because students are more likely to speak some English after having been in a bilingual education program, the tests are less reliable for determining whether a student should be mainstreamed than for determining whether a student should be assigned to the program in the first place. Moreover, even if the tests were in agreement, this would still not mean they were valid—they could just all have the same bias.

Causes of Poor Performance in School

For tests of English language proficiency to be valid, they must be able to distinguish between students who do poorly in school because of the language barrier and those who do poorly in school for other reasons. Rosenthal, Baker, and Ginsburg (1983) demonstrate how unsuccessful these identification methods are in sorting out the various causes of poor school performance.[39]

Using standardized test scores and home language data from parent interviews in a nationally representative sample of 15,000 students in grades 1 through 6, the authors were able to construct procedures analogous to those in the proposed *Lau* regulations, the most detailed and refined procedures ever constructed, and then use them to identify students in need of bilingual education. Once these students were identified, their performance was analyzed to assess the extent to which their low achievement was a result of their non-English language background or the result of other home background factors.

Although the analysis found there was a language background effect on achievement, other family characteristics, such as parental education, occupation, and income, were much more important causes of poor performance in school. These procedures failed to distinguish students who have problems in school because of the language barrier from students who have problems in school for other reasons.

Mayeske et al. (1973) found that among Hispanic students, once socioeconomic status was controlled, the use of Spanish at home had no relationship to achievement in school.[40] While several other studies have found that both language background and other home background factors are related to the educational attainment of Hispanics,[41] the literature in general suggests that non-language factors are much more powerful determinants of poor school performance in language minority students than are language factors. All of these studies suggest how difficult it is to isolate the educational effects of a non-English language background.

THE INCIDENCE OF MISCLASSIFICATION

The logical flaws in the selection methods make it possible for fluent English-speaking students to be taught reading in Spanish (or any other language) on the grounds that this will help them learn English. The next question is, how often does this happen? Here we run into another area in which little research has been done. For the most part, we will have to answer the question with indirect evidence, none of which has been obtained in Massachusetts.

The American Institutes for Research (AIR) national evaluation of Title VII programs, which found that Title VII students were performing worse in English and about the same in math as were non-Title VII students, also found that less than one-third of the students in Title VII classrooms were there because of their need for

English instruction as judged by their classroom teacher. Only 16 percent were monolingual Spanish speakers. When asked what happens to the Spanish-dominant child after he or she is able to function in English, 86 percent of the project directors reported that the child remained in the bilingual project.[42]

The Office of the Inspector General of the US Department of Education found widespread misclassification of students as LEP in Title VII projects in Texas using the identification procedures contained in the Bilingual Education Act.

> Most districts, however, automatically categorized students as LEP even if the home language surveys showed that the child spoke only English and their parents only occasionally spoke Spanish...For example, 812 (53 percent) of the 1,524 LEP-classified students par-ticipating in Edgewood's three Title VII projects were categorized as LEP because they had been designated as underachievers by the district (scoring below the 40th percentile on the Comprehensive Tests of Basic Skills total battery score)...English was the dominant language for most Title VII project participants, including at least 1,378 or 33 [sic] [it is actually 90 percent] percent of the participating LEP students. Most LEP-classified preschool students participating in Austin's demonstration project spoke only English, based on the results of oral language proficiency tests...they were classified as LEP mostly because home language surveys showed that Spanish was sometimes used at home.[43]

Until 1994, Title VII required a minimum of 60 percent LEP enrollment. In the six projects audited, the Inspector General found LEP enrollments of 9 percent, 40 percent, 49 percent, 50 percent, 48 percent, and 58 percent.[44] Although no similar audit has been conducted in Massachusetts, Rossell's conversations with teachers indicate that in any given self-contained classroom there is a small percentage of fluent English speakers who are there solely because of their language minority status and low test scores. This percentage is greater the higher the grade in school so that by fifth grade, half or more of the students in a self-contained classroom may be fluent English speakers.

Along the same lines, Dulay and Burt (1980) found that only half the Hispanic students identified as LEP in a sample of California school districts were more fluent in Spanish than they were in English. In one school district, almost 40 percent of the Hispanic LEP children spoke no Spanish at all. In comparing relative language proficiency to the results of the home language survey in two of the school districts, they found only one-third (362) of the 994 students were Spanish superior. The authors appealed "for greater variety in designing bilingual programs and less legal rigidity in mandating home language instruction."[45]

Illustrative of the problem is a study of relative language proficiency among Hispanic students by Duncan and De Avila (1979).[46] A majority (54) of the 101 students classified by the Language Assessment Scales (LAS), widely used in Massachusetts, as limited or non-proficient in Spanish were also classified as limited or non-proficient in English. Of the 96 students found to be limited or non-proficient in English, less than half (42) were found to be proficient Spanish speakers. Overall, more than half the students in the sample were classified by the LAS as limited or non-proficient in both Spanish and English.

Russell and Ortiz (1989) similarly found the LAS to overclassify students as limited speakers of Spanish and English.[47] They assessed the language proficiency of 23 Hispanic students in three different settings. Only six of the 23 students who were limited in English were classified as Spanish-proficient by the LAS, while three-quarters were classified as not proficient in either language.

Pelavin et al. (1988) estimated that in their entry sample of 1,200 language minority students, using only an oral-language proficiency test misclassified between 12 and 24 percent of the students, depending on the test used. (Misclassification was defined as a classification different from that made by teachers who had been trained for this study to determine language proficiency.) Using multiple indicators, as the school districts in their studies actually did, resulted in less than 8 percent misclassification.

With the exit sample, there was even greater misclassification. Using only an oral language proficiency test misclassified between 28 and 36 percent of the students as LEP and thus kept them from exiting the program.

A 1985 report to Federal District Court Judge Arthur Garrity on TBE in Boston found that 45 percent of the TBE middle school students and 44 percent of high school TBE students had been kept in the program for six years or more without ever obtaining an English language score high enough to allow them to exit.[48] Only 2 percent of the elementary bilingual education students had scored high enough in English to begin the process of mainstreaming into regular English-speaking classrooms. Although the implication of the report is that most students were not exited because they were not learning English in their bilingual education classes, it is at least as probable that the exit test could not distinguish between a student's lack of English proficiency and his or her general low achievement in any language.[49]

In addition, the language proficiency tests are not easy to pass even for high achieving students. The Chicago Board of Education administered the LAS to students who spoke *only English* and were *above* the citywide ITBS norms in reading.[50] Almost half of these monolingual, above-average, English-speaking children were misclassified by the test as non- or limited-English-speaking. Moreover, there is a developmental trend. The correlation between age and percentage of monolingual English-speaking children classified as LEP by the test is -.66. Seventy-eight percent of the five-year-olds, but only 25 percent of the 14-year-olds, were classified as LEP.

The tests not only misclassify students as LEP for placement in bilingual education, they skew the statistics on how many LEP students there are in the nation. The National Institute of Edu-cation developed the Language Measurement and Assessment Instrument (LM&AI) and administered the test to a stratified random sample of students. Students who took the test were then classified as LEP or FEP based on their test scores. From this, statistical estimating procedures were used to determine that there were 3.6 million LEP students in the nation in 1981.[51] Barnes (1983) reanalyzed these data and found that two-thirds, or 2.4 million, of these students spoke English as their dominant language.[52] Similarly, Berdan et al. (1982) administered the LM&AI to Cherokee students at the request of the Cherokee Nation, which wanted to determine the need for Cherokee bilingual education. Through home interviews, Berdan et al. found that 82 percent of the Cherokee students were English monolinguals. The LM&AI, however, classified 48 percent of these monolingual English-speaking children as LEP.[53]

In 1984, the U.S. Department of Education had the LM&AI administered to a nationally representative sample of monolingual English-speaking school-aged children. The test classified 42 percent of these English monolingual students as limited in English.[54]

TEACHER JUDGMENT

The procedures we have been discussing were developed as an improvement on teacher judgment. Therefore, it is worth exploring how they compare. It should be noted that outside the field of educational equity, teacher ratings are generally preferred to test scores.

Although teacher ratings correlate highly with standardized achievement tests,[55] they are considered more accurate in assessing functional aspects of children's classroom performance than are tests and thus more useful for instructional purposes.[56]

Ulibarri et al. (1980, 1981) analyzed teacher rating, achievement test data, and oral language proficiency from five school districts in a sample of 900 first, third, and fifth grade students. The children were administered the Comprehensive Test of Basic Skills (CTBS), California Achievement Test (CAT), and Stanford Achievement Test (SAT), and the LAS, BSM, and BINL oral language proficiency tests. Three pieces of teacher rating information were related to achievement test scores: 1) English language proficiency, 2) competency in reading and math, and 3) chance for achievement if instructed in English. The teacher rating variables and the language proficiency scores on the LAS, BSM, and BINL were entered into a step-wise multiple regression analysis to predict academic achievement in reading and math. Across grades, teacher variables were the best predictors of reading and math achievement, explaining 41 percent of the variance. The BINL, BSM, and LAS showed relatively poor correlations and added 0 percent, 1 percent, and 4 percent respectively to the prediction of actual achievement. Moreover, the authors noted their findings were consistent with other studies, which also found teacher variables to be the best predictors of academic achievement in several different Spanish language groups.

The Southwest Educational Development Laboratory's (SEDL) seven-year longitudinal study of the reading progress of 800 children in grades K-4 used a different methodology to come to similar conclusions. Language assessment data were collected using three types of measures: 1) the LAS oral language proficiency instrument, 2) teacher ratings of students' language proficiency, and 3) "ethnographic verification" of the children's language abilities from half-hour monthly audiotaped samples of free speech in three settings—the classroom, playground, and family.[57] Teacher ratings of proficiency were highly related to the linguistic analyses of taped free speech of the same children. Most importantly, the LAS rated the children's proficiency in both Spanish and English as significantly lower than either teacher ratings or linguistic analysis, classifying children as non- or limited speakers in either language when native teacher judgment indicated native or near-native proficiency.[58]

Russell and Ortiz (1989) produced similar results. They found that the English LAS did not predict English language proficiency in spontaneous conversation nor did it predict reading achievement. Indeed, the best predictor of reading achievement was the teacher's rating of language proficiency, which explained almost all of the variation—43 percent out of a total of 59 percent. They concluded that,

> If the LAS and the Pre-LAS do not predict language competence in spontaneous conversations or reading achievement, they are of limited value in making placement decisions or planning educational programs for LEP students.[59]

These studies thus indicate that teacher judgments are better predictors of both language proficiency and academic achievement than standardized language proficiency tests. Teachers and administrators believe this as well. In a survey conducted in 1979, the Southwest Regional Laboratory for Educational Research and Development found the collective experience of these test users to be quite discouraging.

> ...They expressed little confidence in the tests. Generally users felt that teacher judgment was more likely to be a valid measure of both language proficiency and capability of succeeding in an all-English-medium classroom than any test that they had been using. However, project staff had continued to employ the tests in the entry/exit process in order to satisfy

> state or federal regulations or to give the appearance of objectivity in project decision making.[60]

We must ask, then, what is the point of prescribing elaborate surveys and testing programs to replace teacher judgment when the empirical literature and practical experience indicate that teacher judgment is more accurate?

CONCLUSION

Our conclusion is straightforward: policymakers require identification and assessment procedures that do not accomplish their goal. Indeed, they are less accurate than what they were intended to replace—teacher judgment.

Theoretically, a child who needs bilingual education or some other form of special language help is one who is having problems in English but speaks another language. A child who needs compensatory education, on the other hand, is one who is having problems in English and speaks no other language competently. Unfortunately, there are no English language proficiency tests currently in existence that can distinguish between these two types of students. Yet these tests are required or recommended throughout the United States. To its credit, the Massachusetts Department of Education strongly recommends a holistic assessment approach in which tests are only one element. A more accurate assessment process, however, would explicitly recognize the specific limitations of each test or eliminate the tests altogether.

CHAPTER SIX

THE COST OF TRANSITIONAL BILINGUAL EDUCATION

No one knows exactly how much education programs for LEP students cost.[1] These programs are rarely, if ever, a single bookkeeping line item, and even when they are the line item never captures all relevant costs. This makes it very difficult to track the cost of any particular program. The best chance for estimating the cost of a particular program comes when it is funded entirely through a categorical grant with an accounting requirement attached to it. If it can be assumed that no other funds contribute to the program (normally a questionable assumption), it can be costed out reasonably accurately. As the number of funding sources increases, it becomes more difficult to figure out what the program costs; different sources have different reporting requirements, and money is commingled in the process of paying school expenses. Moreover, money specifically earmarked for a particular program is not necessarily spent on that program alone.

Is it possible to measure with precision the cost of bilingual education? Given the state of existing accounting practices in virtually all school districts, the answer is no. With effort, however, it is possible to develop sophisticated estimates on a small scale that can provide enough data for policymakers and school officials to make informed decisions.

We can draw one conclusion about cost from our general knowledge of how these programs and school systems work: bilingual education programs—those programs that include native tongue instruction in a self-contained classroom—will cost more than the regular classroom program. Bilingual programs may also cost more than some all-English alternatives for LEP students.

The reasons bilingual programs, such as the Spanish TBE programs in Massachusetts that operate in accordance with Chapter 71A, cost more than regular education are straightforward: First, bilingual programs need two sets of instructional materials, one in each language. Second, they typically have—and often are required to have—smaller classes. In Massachusetts, for example, the TBE regulations require that,

> Except for multi-grade level classes (classes in which more than one grade level is/are included), the maximum student-teacher ratio shall be 18:1, except that the student-teacher ratio may be 25:1, where a native speaking teacher's aide is assigned to a Transitional Bilingual Education class or a non-native teacher's aide is assigned to a Transitional Bilingual Education class taught by a native speaker of the primary language of the children enrolled in the Transitional Bilingual Education program. In multi-grade level classes, as defined supra, the ratio shall be 15:1 without said aide and 20:1 with said aide, respectively.[2]

Third, any education program that requires a separate staff and administrative oversight will add a layer of bureaucracy to the school's and school district's existing administrative structures, making total administrative costs greater than they would be otherwise.

When education programs are mandated by state and/or federal law, the costs of maintaining federal and state bureaucracies, administering funding and policy development programs, and monitoring compliance should also be considered part of the overall costs of the program. Few, if any, of the analyses that have been done have included all costs incurred at the state and federal levels.

Cost Analysis Methods

There are three basic methods used to analyze costs of education programs, each of which addresses different policy issues: 1) the total program cost method, 2) the added cost method, and 3) the comparative cost method. These may be applied at the district level and include all the district's programs for LEP students or at the school level to compare different programs within the district.

Total Program Cost

The total program cost approach determines how much a year of schooling costs for the students in the program being studied. The policy question is simply how much the district is spending on the program. The answer can be given as either a per-pupil cost or the total for all students in the program. A total program cost analysis of TBE will include the full salary of the classroom teacher as part of the cost of the program, ignoring the fact that the school would incur most of these costs if the student were not in a TBE program. The total cost analysis is useful as a political tool to impress voters, politicians, or special interest groups with how much the school district is doing for LEP students because it produces the largest value for the cost of the program. For the same reason, it is a useful political tool for critics of bilingual education.

Added Program Cost

The more important policy question is what it costs to operate the program *over and above* the cost of educating students who are not in the program. The added cost analysis is a standard economic approach whose major drawback is its complexity. The added cost of a TBE program (or of any program) is calculated by subtracting the cost of the regular instructional program[3] from the cost of the TBE program. If the TBE program uses instructional materials in two languages or has an identifiable administrative structure within the school district bureaucracy, an added cost analysis will usually find the bilingual education program to be more expensive than the regular classroom program.

COMPARATIVE PROGRAM COST

A comparative cost analysis would look at the relative costs of two or more programs designed to meet the special needs of LEP students. This is the method to use if a school district is considering replacing a TBE program with a structured immersion program, for example. It answers the question of what happens to the cost of teaching LEP students if the school changes programs. A comparative cost analysis can be done by computing the total cost of each alternative program and then comparing them, or it can be done by computing the added costs of each program and then comparing those costs.

COST ESTIMATES FOR BILINGUAL EDUCATION

The American Legislative Exchange Council (ALEC) and U.S. English (1994) statistics purport to estimate the cost of bilingual education in the United States in 1991-92.[4] In fact, however, all they did was to take statistics on the number of LEP students in each state in each type of program—bilingual education, ESL, and "unknown"[5]—and then multiply that figure times the average per-pupil expenditure in the state for that year. The effect of this shorthand calculation is to assume away any differences between programs in per-pupil expenditures. According to their data, about $5.5 billion is spent on programs called bilingual education, and $1.9 billion is spent on ESL by state and local governments. ALEC and US English also note that $84,031,000 was given to the states by the federal government (Title VII) for bilingual education (both transitional and developmental), and $32,156,000 was awarded for special alternative programs in English in FY 92. If we add these federal funds (about $116 million) to the state and local funds, the total spent on programs called bilingual education is about $5.63 billion. The grand total federal, state, and local spending for all programs for LEP students (including bilingual education, ESL, and "unknown") is a little more than $10 billion.

The report also ranks states by estimated state and local per-pupil expenditures for "bilingual education." Massachusetts is ranked 7th in the nation and is, relative to other states, a big spender because it has a lot of LEP students in bilingual education programs.

The ALEC estimate for state and local expenditures in Massachusetts was $241,991,523 for 38,043 LEP students in bilingual education in 1991-92, a per-pupil expenditure of $6,361. The data reported by Massachusetts school districts to the state, albeit for the following year, yields an average per-pupil expenditure of $4,870, almost $1,500 lower than ALEC's estimate.[6]

Carpenter-Huffman and Samulon (1981, 1983) conducted a fairly sophisticated added cost analysis, although not at the level we would like to see.[7] They underestimated the cost of self-contained bilingual education programs by accepting the lower average salaries of the bilingual teachers, who had less experience than the others, as a savings to the program (see discussion below). They calculated the added cost of bilingual education to range from $200 to $700 in the six districts they analyzed. But they defined bilingual education more broadly than we do. They include in their definition all programs for LEP students. They found that the difference between school districts was in large part a function of the type of instructional delivery system the school district had—they found ESL pullout programs to be more expensive than self-contained TBE programs. Self-contained programs, the only ones with native tongue instruction, had more expensive materials.[8] But because teachers' salaries are a greater expense than instructional materials, the pullout programs were more expensive; in these programs each LEP student had more than one teacher—a regular classroom teacher and part of an ESL teacher. Therefore, in their analysis, programs for LEP students were more expensive than a regular education, but bilingual education in a self-contained classroom was less expensive than ESL pullout.

Cardenas, Bernal, and Kean (1976) used a "judgmental cost model" to estimate the added costs of a "minimally adequate" hypothetical bilingual education program. Their estimate of the added cost ranged from 30 to 35 percent of regular education in Texas, from 17 to 25 percent in Utah, and from 15 to 22 percent in Colorado.[9]

Garcia (1977) analyzed add-on costs of existing bilingual education programs in New Mexico.[10] These costs included teacher aides' salaries, direct program administration, supplies, and materials. Bilingual teachers' salaries were added only if the teachers were specifically hired as bilingual teachers. The pupil-teacher ratios were about the same in bilingual education as in regularly provided education in his sample. Calculated add-on costs totaled $205 per pupil or 27 percent more than the cost of regular education.

Prince and Hubert (1990) estimated the additional cost of bilingual education in Hartford, Connecticut, to be about $680 per pupil, or about 15 percent of per-pupil costs.[11] They argued that a general, simplified estimate could also be obtained by collecting only salary-related expenses, since costs other than salaries represented only 5 percent of the total cost in their analysis.

All of these studies made a good faith effort to calculate the added cost of bilingual education. However, in each case the discussion of methodology was too brief and too simple to offer assurance that they were actually successful.

TBE Expenditures Reported by Massachusetts Districts

Appendix 6-1 shows a ranking of Massachusetts TBE districts by the difference between what each district reported for per-pupil expenditures on regular programs and on TBE.[12] These differences are based on total cost estimates and cannot be considered accurate added cost analyses, or accurate answers to the relevant policy question—what is spent on TBE over and above the regular education program? The state conducts workshops and each year sends out a 35- to 50-page booklet to the school districts on what to put into the various categories of the reporting form, but there are no instructions on *how* to estimate the cost of specific programs. As a result, the estimates given by the school districts to the state vary wildly, and many of them clearly are in error.

As we look down the data in appendix 6-1, we see some extreme outliers—school districts whose per-pupil expenditures for bilingual education are nearly $10,000 more than their per-pupil expenditures for regular education. At the opposite end of the spectrum are those school districts that report spending as much as $4,000 *less* for bilingual education than they do for regular education. This is impossible if they are in any way following the content of the law and the regulations. We are quite familiar with several of these school districts, and there is no way they can provide the additional services they offer to LEP students for less money than is being spent on regular students. Therefore, the only conclusion that one can draw is that for individual school districts, these expenditure data are unreliable even for very simple total cost analyses.

We are struck, however, by how close the *average* additional expenditure for bilingual education reported by these districts of $1,179—25 percent more than regular education—is to the added cost analyses that have been conducted in a more rigorous way by researchers.

ESTIMATING THE COST OF TBE IN MASSACHUSETTS

The first step in a cost analysis of TBE is deciding what specific issue to address and which type of analysis best addresses that issue. In the course of the analysis, many decisions will have to be made about how to treat different cost factors, and the reason for the study is a major determinant of those decisions.

For example, a school district may get $1 million from Title VII, the US Department of Education's bilingual education program; $100,000 from a state bilingual education program; and $1 million of local money for bilingual education—a total of $2.1 million that can only be spent for the district's TBE program. But the school district also gets $2 million for the US Department of Education's Title I program for poor students, and 30 percent of these funds are used to help LEP students learn English. Should the total cost of the TBE program include the cost of all programs for LEP students, including those in Title I? The answer to this question depends on why the cost analysis is being done.

If the LEP students are in a self-contained TBE classroom, is the teacher's salary a cost of the program? The school would have provided a teacher for these students if there were no TBE program. Is it fair to charge the TBE program for something that is provided to all students? But what if the TBE program requires a teacher with special training or certification that makes her more expensive than mainstream teachers? Or if a TBE program has smaller classes than the regular instruction program? How are these costs analyzed?

In the remainder of this chapter, we discuss how one would calculate the added cost of TBE compared to the regular classroom. We assume the TBE program is implemented according to chapter 71A and includes instruction in the native language. If the reader wants to know the comparative costs of other special programs for LEP children, this same added cost analysis should be performed for those programs. If the intent is to choose between special programs for LEP children, then their added costs should be compared.

Guidelines for Conducting an Added Cost Analysis

Two important guidelines must be followed in any cost analysis:

• First, the costs of *equivalent levels* of services must be compared. For example, it is misleading to compare the cost of a program that provides special help in both language and math for a total of four hours a day to the cost of a program that provides only one hour a day of such help in math, without standardizing the costs to create a fair comparison. Other cases are more subtle, however, and the necessity of comparing only equivalent levels of services is not so apparent.

• Second, only factors *unique* to the program should be counted in the cost difference between the two programs.

Teachers

Consider the cost of teachers. Seldom will the actual cost of regular classroom teachers and TBE teachers be exactly the same. Determining why the costs are different is critical.

The salary schedules of most school systems reward teachers who have additional education and those with more teaching experience. If the school district requires, or prefers to hire, state-certified bilingual education teachers, and this certification requires additional education, then the salary differential between a teacher with a BA and one with an advanced certificate is counted as a cost to the TBE program. On the other hand, if the school district requires a similar number of courses for all its teachers, then there is no real added cost for the teachers in the bilingual education program. In most states, bilingual certified teachers must have more years of college education or an advanced degree not required of regular classroom teachers and as a result are paid more than regular classroom teachers with the same years of teaching experience.

Since bilingual education programs have been in existence for a relatively short time, bilingual education teachers often are younger and have less teaching experience than the rest of the teaching force, which places them, all other things being equal, lower on the salary scale. Some bilingual education advocates have asserted that because bilingual education teachers earn less than regular classroom teachers, bilingual education is a bargain for the schools. But, if at each level of teaching experience, the bilingual teacher is paid more because of additional education required by the program, the bilingual teachers are in reality more expensive than regular teachers even though the average salary of bilingual teachers may be lower because as a group they have less teaching experience.[13]

If teachers for TBE programs are recruited separately from regular classroom teachers, then the costs of recruiting both types of teachers must be included in the cost analysis. If bonuses are paid to TBE teachers, as is the case in Los Angeles, all the costs associated with the bonus must be counted in the TBE program cost.

Classroom Aides

Unless it is the school's practice that all regular classrooms have an aide as well as a teacher, the full cost of the aides assigned to the TBE program should be counted in the program cost. If some regular classrooms have aides, then the added cost for TBE is the difference between the per-pupil expenditures for aides in the regular program and the per-pupil expenditure in the bilingual program.

Fringe Benefits

In addition to staff salaries, fringe benefits, which can be considerable in school systems, must be charged for all staff time devoted to the program. Since only that part of the teacher's salary which is an added cost is attributed to the program, only a comparable proportion of fringe benefits should be assigned to the program. However, for administrative or other staff time spent on the bilingual education program, full fringe benefits for that period of time should be included. Fringe benefits include the employer contribution to social security, any other retirement program paid for by the school district or the state, health insurance, other insurance provided by the district, stipends for further education, and the annualized pro-rated cost of sabbaticals.

Administrative Costs

All administrative costs connected with the program are added program costs. These include administrators explicitly assigned to the TBE program and all time spent on TBE by all other school administrative staff. For example, when the principal works on the TBE program, that time is taken away from other programs at the school, which is a loss to these other programs. Consequently, it is a cost charged to the TBE program. This is true of time spent by all administrators, psychologists, guidance counselors, etc., on problems that are unique to the TBE program.

If the school's general enrollment documents ask all students questions about language background, then the staff time needed to get the answers to these questions for all students is a cost of any special program for LEP students because it would not be done if the school did not have these special programs. Likewise, all costs associated with testing or otherwise screening students for placement in the program are part of the program costs.

In comparing different programs for LEP students to each other, this added cost will often be the same for each one. If, however, the TBE program requires testing in both Spanish and English, and the other programs for LEP children require testing only in English because no native tongue instruction will be used, then the cost of testing in Spanish will make the added cost of the TBE program higher than the added cost of the other special programs.

Textbooks and Instructional Material

Any instructional material used that is over and above what is provided to mainstream students is a program cost. If the students in the TBE program are given the same set of English-language texts as mainstream students, there is no program cost for these books. If bilingual students are also given a set of instructional materials in either another language, or a set of bilingual instructional materials that are not provided to mainstream students, these additional materials count as a cost of the program, even if they are sometimes used in place of the mainstream materials. If, however, instructional materials in one language completely supplant those in another language for one year, then there is little or no additional cost. For example, a TBE program that uses nothing but Spanish materials for the first year and nothing but English materials for the last year would have no additional costs for those years, unless the Spanish materials were more expensive than comparable English texts.

The same issues must also be addressed for other types of instructional materials—audio visual materials, trade books, reference materials, art supplies, etc.

Library

All bilingual books in the library and all books written in a language other than English should be charged to the cost of the TBE program unless these books are also used by English-speaking students not in the program who are studying that language as a second language. In that case, the cost of the non-English language books should be split between the two programs in proportion to the total number of students enrolled in each program.[14] The same rules apply to all other non-English language media in the library. A part of the library staff's salary and fringe benefits proportionate to either the amount of non-English language media or the staff time devoted to these materials is also a cost of the program.

Transportation

Transportation costs for TBE may be substantial if students are bused to a central location for TBE classes. If TBE is provided in a student's neighborhood school, transportation to school, which the student would have received anyway, should not be charged to the cost of the program.

We know that in at least one TBE program students stay 45 minutes longer than the regular school day.[15] Consequently, buses have to make two trips. The full cost of running a second bus trip is charged to the program unless there is already a second bus trip for regular students.

Class Size

If there is a difference in the average class size between TBE classes and regular classes, it is counted in the cost of the TBE program. There are several steps involved in calculating the added cost of reduced class size. The first step is to calculate the added cost of a TBE teacher.[16] To do this, one must compare the requirements and pay scale for these teachers to the requirements and pay scale for regular classroom teachers. If there is no difference in the educational requirements for teachers in the two programs, or no difference in the salary paid to teachers with the average education of those in each program, the added cost of a TBE teacher would be $0. If there are differences in educational requirements and in the salary scale, the salaries paid to each type of teacher at an equal level of education and teaching experience can be used to compare teacher costs. Take the average regular teacher salary and then determine the salary that would be paid to a bilingual education teacher with the same education and years of experience. The second step is to determine the per-pupil teacher salary in each program by dividing the average regular teacher salary by the average number of students in a regular classroom and the comparable bilingual teacher salary by the average number of students in a bilingual classroom. The third step in this process is to multiply the total number of students in the bilingual education program by the per-pupil bilingual teacher salary. The fourth step is to calculate what it would cost to educate these same students in a regular classroom by multiplying the total number of students in the regular program by the per-pupil regular teacher salary. To determine the added cost of reduced class size, compare the per-pupil cost in bilingual education (from step three) to the per-pupil cost in the regular classroom (from step four).

Classroom Integration

Some school districts assign or recruit a number of native English-speaking students into the TBE classroom to compensate for the segregation by ethnicity that often occurs in self-contained bilingual education classrooms. Some analysts argue that because the school would have to teach these children if they were not in the TBE program, none of the costs of their education should be assigned to TBE. This is incorrect, however, if the TBE program creates added costs for teaching these students that would not be incurred if they were placed in a regular classroom setting. If English-speaking students in the TBE program are receiving Spanish instruction, textbooks, and materials that they would not receive in the regular classroom, those materials are a cost of TBE. If they are also in a smaller classroom, then that added cost should be assigned to the TBE program. The cost of TBE is not just the cost of instructing LEP students in a TBE classroom—it is the cost of instructing *all* students who are in this instructional program.

Dual Eligibility

Another problem encountered in assessing the cost of TBE programs involves students who are eligible for more than one program. Almost all LEP students are also eligible for Title I, but individual students are rarely found in both programs. Schools often compensate for lack of funding by limiting students to one special program each. If a student in the bilingual education program is also eligible for another program, does the comparative cost of teaching him in the bilingual education program include a savings from not placing him in the other program? In most cases, the answer is no. Even if the student is taken out of bilingual education and placed in the regular program, it does not necessarily follow that he or she would then be assigned to Title I.

A good case can be made that "compensatory programs" are not part of the regular classroom program and should never be included in the computation of the cost of the regular classroom. If this approach is taken, the costs of all these programs must be removed when calculating the cost of the regular classroom program.

Below are two approaches that can be used for doing a complete added cost analysis. These same procedures can be used in a complete total cost or complete comparative cost analysis.

THE COST OF STANDARD SERVICES

This is by far the most accurate and most difficult way to compute the cost of bilingual education programs. Those who want to calculate accurately the cost of bilingual education programs should consult Harget (1978), where the procedure is clearly laid out in detail.[17] The essence of the procedure is to compare the cost of the package of educational services received by the students in the bilingual education program to the package of services they would receive if they were not in the program.

A student's educational program is determined not only by enrollment in bilingual education. There is considerable variation between programs and between classrooms within the same program, as well as within the regular classroom. To assess accurately any particular student's educational program, it is necessary to conduct extensive classroom observations mapping the package of services each student receives. Once the service packages received by the students are recorded, the cost of each service provided is calculated. Then the cost of each student's program package is computed by adding up the costs of all the services he or she receives. The individual costs per student are then totaled to get the program cost. Then the added or comparative costs are calculated.

ESTIMATING THE COST OF THE PROGRAM BY ASKING WHO NEEDS IT

Asking who needs a program is a shortcut that might produce reasonably accurate results with a lot less work than it takes to do a standard services/added cost analysis. This shortcut is based on a simple proposition: if mainstream students need a service, it isn't a cost of the TBE program. Another way to think of it is to imagine all the LEP students magically mastered English overnight and could be mainstreamed. Everything you would throw away or store away or not buy in the future to convert their classes to mainstream classes is a cost of the TBE program. Keeping this idea in mind will help guide the analyst in deciding what is and what isn't a cost of TBE.

CONCLUSION

Given the complexity of analyzing the cost of bilingual education, an added cost analysis has to be done on a case study basis. The most accurate case study would include extensive classroom observation and administrator and teacher interviews. We began such a study but found the task of correctly calculating the added cost of bilingual education impossible within our time and budgetary constraints. School budgets are not organized to enable analysts to calculate opportunity costs and the package of services that a student receives.

Two alternative and perhaps complementary accounting techniques could greatly improve the usefulness of school spending data for researchers and school officials alike. The first is Activity-Based Costing (ABC). ABC is an accounting tool that identifies costs on an outcomes basis. It is finding growing acceptance in business and municipal government. ABC allocates the cost of all inputs necessary to produce a single unit of output. For instance, using ABC a municipality can determine the average cost of filling a pothole. Similarly, ABC might be used by a school district to determine the cost of teaching a single student to read English at a fourth grade level.

Another promising tool is the Finance Analysis Model™ (FAM), which is being developed by Coopers and Lybrand and the US Chamber of Commerce's Center for Workforce Preparation. FAM is a PC-based software product that converts general ledger data into a standardized budgetary framework, organized by function, program (including bilingual education), and location.

The cost analyses that have been done appear to provide a rough estimate of the cost of existing programs for LEP students. Taking into account all the data available, it appears that "bilingual education," here broadly defined to include all special programs for LEP students, costs between $200 and $1,000 more than regular education. While one study found ESL pullout programs to be more expensive than self-contained bilingual education programs, that study had unusually large TBE classrooms of 31 students and ESL pullout classes of nine. If we assume a self-contained TBE classroom of 18 compared to a regular classroom of 31 students with an ESL pullout class of nine students for 1/6 of each day, the TBE classroom is still less expensive.[18] However, if one increases the ESL class size to 12 and decreases the TBE class size to 13, still much larger than the triggering point in Massachusetts of 1 to 2 students per grade (i.e., 20 LEP students of a single language group in a district), the TBE program will be more expensive. Thus, while a pullout program will often be less expensive than a self-contained classroom, the cost difference depends on class sizes and the presence of aides.

Appendix 6-1
Ranking of Massachusetts Districts by Difference in Reported Per-Pupil Expenditures in TBE and Regular Programs, 1992–1993

DISTRICT	$ TBE– $ Regular	TBE Enrollment
Randolph	9,897	129
Barnstable	8,530	0
Medford	6,575	94
Stoughton	4,278	19
Revere	4,085	241
Northampton	3,888	98
Scituate	3,593	29
New Bedford	3,437	821
Marlborough	3,376	36
Peabody	3,151	65
Boston	2,755	11915
Newton	2,735	327
Hudson	2,637	0
Fitchburg	2,221	412
Lynn	1,869	1382
Attleboro	1,839	77
Worcester	1,538	1351
Cambridge	1,440	711
Fall River	1,359	902
Ludlow	1,316	40
Taunton	1,250	332
Brockton	1,087	1053
Lowell	886	3100
Waltham	883	220
Westfield	857	273
Haverhill	608	297
Watertown	509	21
Amherst	413	72
Somerville	212	793
Quincy	186	108

Appendix 6-1 (cont'd)
Ranking of Massachusetts Districts by Difference in Reported Per-Pupil Expenditures in TBE and Regular Programs, 1992–1993

DISTRICT	$ TBE– $ Regular	TBE Enrollment
Milford	177	226
Lawrence	142	3849
Methuen	(466)	401
Clinton	(475)	64
Chelsea	(482)	687
Leominster	(747)	158
Holyoke	(1,056)	2300
Salem	(1,063)	576
West Springfield	(1,135)	100
Framingham	(1,193)	550
Brookline	(1,547)	495
Amherst-Pelham	(1,614)	45
Chicopee	(1,833)	529
Southbridge	(2,066)	200
Lexington	(2,271)	22
Malden	(2,363)	432
Springfield	(4,022)	2709
AVERAGE	1,179	
RANGE	13,919	

Source: Massachusetts Department of Education, 1992-93. Preliminary Per-Pupil Expenditures by Program.

Note: Figures in parentheses indicate reported expenditures on TBE were lower than expenditures for regular education.

CHAPTER SEVEN

OPINION SURVEYS

Parental preferences for educating children who do not speak English is of more than academic interest. Liberals, who generally support bilingual education programs, argue that such programs are in part justified because they are desired by the language minority community. Conservatives, who usually oppose bilingual education programs, strongly support the idea of parental choice in schooling. Thus, if language minority parents show strong support for bilingual education, this might serve as common ground for the two camps and a basis for educational policy. If language minority parents feel strongly that the public schools should teach their children literacy in their native language, even at the expense of their English language proficiency, that would be an important justification for offering bilingual education to children whose parents want it.

Originally we were going to interview by telephone parents of LEP students who were enrolled in public schools in Massachusetts. These parents were to be drawn randomly from a list of telephone numbers of LEP children obtained from school district records. We were unable to do this, however, because Massachusetts Education, Training and Advocacy, Inc. (META), a Hispanic advocacy group in Somerville, sent a letter to every school district in the state threatening legal action if any cooperated with our parent survey. Apparently, META does not want to know the opinions of parents of LEP children in Massachusetts as it has been unwilling to do its own survey. Without telephone numbers of LEP children from school district records, locating their parents would be prohibitively expensive.[1]

THE SURVEYS

As a substitute for conducting our own survey in Massachusetts we analyze in this chapter the results of other surveys of parental and adult attitudes toward bilingual education programs conducted over the last 15 years. These surveys polled a variety of respondent groups, including adults nationwide and in specific geographic areas, non-Hispanic adults only, registered voters, language minority parents, and parents of LEP children.

The most important of these surveys was contracted by the U.S. Department of Education to the Educational Testing Service (ETS) in 1988.[2] The ETS survey asked a number of questions that, in one way or another, elicited language minority parents' opinions of bilingual education programs. Depending on the question, the favorable response toward bilingual education programs ranged from over 80 percent to less than 1 percent, a staggering difference in magnitude.

An even more striking aspect of the ETS and other surveys is the logical inconsistencies in the way parents answered the questions. For example, in the ETS survey, 70 percent of the parents said they wanted the school to teach literacy in both languages. But only 12 percent of Mexican-American parents wanted Spanish taught in school *if* it meant less time for teaching English, and no more than 22 percent were willing to reduce art or music. At a minimum, 42 to 52 percent of Mexican-American parents wanted no reduction in English or any other subject in order to *include* Spanish, *and* they wanted the schools to teach literacy in both languages! They seemed not to consider that adding a second language to the curriculum within the constraints of a fixed school day meant that the use of English in the classroom would decline. Clearly the way a question is worded can dramatically affect the answer.

The trade-off problem—that in the real world of limited resources, more of something usually means less of something else—is an essential but nevertheless neglected question in opinion surveys of preferences. Surveys show that most Americans forget this unless specifically asked what they would be willing to have less of in return for more of the good or service they want. Their answers change dramatically when the trade-off question is asked, usually in the direction of less support for the good or service they originally wanted.

This is evident in the polls about bilingual education, which when the trade-off question is not asked overestimate support for native tongue instruction. We know this because when the trade-off question *is* asked support plummets about 60 points. When the trade-off question is not asked, many parents will express support for policy alternatives that are mutually exclusive. Keeping these problems in mind, we review below a number of surveys conducted over the last 15 years.

Phi Delta Kappan Poll

A Phi Delta Kappan poll conducted in September 1988 of 2,118 adults nationwide asked the following question about bilingual education and got the responses shown below.

[TRANSITIONAL BILINGUAL EDUCATION]

Q: Would you favor or oppose the local public schools' providing instruction in a student's native language, whatever it is, in order to help him or her become a more successful learner?

Favor	42%
Oppose	49
Don't Know	9

INSTITUTE FOR SOCIAL INQUIRY POLL

The Institute for Social Inquiry conducted a poll of 500 Connecticut adults in February 1987.

[NATIVE TONGUE V. ENGLISH]

Q: There are children in Connecticut who speak a language other than English at home. Do you think elementary school subjects for such children should be taught in English, or should they be taught those subjects in their own language while they are learning English?

Taught in English	72%
Taught in own language	26
Don't know	2

[BILINGUAL EDUCATION]

Q: Overall, do you think *bilingual education* helps students to learn English or does it make it harder for them to learn it?

Helps to learn English	36%
Makes it harder	50
Neither	4
Don't know	9

ROPER POLL

The Roper Poll (1982) surveyed language minority parents nationwide and found that native tongue instruction was a relatively low priority for them.[3]

[BILINGUAL MAINTENANCE]

Q: We should have two sets of classes all the way through high school—English speaking classes for the children who speak English, and Spanish speaking classes for the children who speak Spanish.

Agree	9%

[TRANSITIONAL BILINGUAL EDUCATION]

Q: We should have *Spanish speaking classes* for a year or two for the children who speak Spanish while they are learning to speak English, and all English classes from then on.

Agree	39%

[ENGLISH-ONLY EDUCATION]

Q: We should have *only English* speaking classes in our public schools, with Spanish speaking students required to learn English right from the start.

Agree	48%

More language minority parents prefer all English programs than prefer transitional bilingual education. These parents overwhelmingly reject bilingual maintenance programs.

Media General/Associated Press Poll

The Media General/Associated Press Poll #9, a nationwide poll of 1,462 adults conducted in November 1985, found the following:

[BILINGUAL EDUCATION]

Q: On the issue of bilingual education, the traditional method of teaching non-English-speaking children has been to offer the basic classes like math and social studies in their own language while they are taught English in a separate class. In your opinion, do you think this method of *bilingual education* has generally been successful or not successful in *teaching the basic subjects like math and social studies* to non-English speaking students?

Successful	38%
Not successful	23
Don't know	39

[BILINGUAL EDUCATION]

Q: Do you think the traditional method of bilingual education has generally been successful or not successful in teaching these students to speak English?

Successful	42%
Not successful	24
Don't know	34

[NATIVE TONGUE V. ALL ENGLISH]

Q: Do you think non-English-speaking students should be taught basic subjects in their own language while they learn English or should they be placed in all English speaking classes?

Own language	36%
All English	46
Don't know	18

This survey once again illustrates the problems with opinion polls on bilingual education. Almost 40 percent of the respondents don't know whether bilingual education is successful. This is certainly reasonable since this is a very complex policy area and of low salience to many adults. Nevertheless, only 18 percent of the respondents lacked an opinion on whether non-English-speaking students should learn their native language in school. In other words, it appears that some of the respondents who had no opinion on the efficacy of bilingual education were nevertheless willing to express a preference.

GALLUP POLL

The Gallup Poll conducted in 1991 asked 995 registered voters their opinion on bilingual education.[4]

[BILINGUAL MAINTENANCE]

Q: Some people say that our public schools should be responsible for maintaining the languages and cultures that people bring with them to the United States. Others say that this is a private concern and not the responsibility of the public schools. Which comes closer to your view?

All Respondents	
Private concern	71%
Public School's Responsibility	23

Families with a Non-English Language	
Private concern	64%
Public School's Responsibility	29

[TRANSITIONAL BILINGUAL V. BILINGUAL MAINTENANCE]

Q: Bilingual education programs teach children who do not speak English basic subjects such as math or science in their native language, while also teaching them to speak English. Some people feel these bilingual programs should only be used until the child learns English. Others feel bilingual education should continue to be used in order to maintain the native language of these children. Which opinion comes closer to your view?

All Respondents	
Until child learns English	54%
Maintain native language	37

Families with a Non-English Language	
Until child learns English	55%
Maintain native language	36

While fewer than 40 percent of the respondents think bilingual education should be used to maintain the native language of children who do not speak English, even this probably overestimates support since parents are not asked about the "cost" of this maintenance in terms of reduced time spent on other subjects.

Berkeley Survey

The Berkeley Unified School District conducted a survey of 106 Asian and 122 Hispanic parents of elementary LEP children who were enrolled in either a regular classroom with ESL pullout or a transitional bilingual education program.[5] Among these parents, 44 percent preferred a bilingual program in which their child would be instructed partly in his or her primary language and partly in English. Forty-nine percent preferred the regular classroom with ESL pullout.

There were fairly large differences, however, between the opinions of Asian and Hispanic parents. Whereas 65 percent of Hispanic parents preferred a bilingual program, only 34 percent of Asian parents did. This more or less mirrors enrollment in the two programs. Most Asian parents of LEP children had their child enrolled in a regular classroom with ESL pullout—even the "Chinese" bilingual program at one school was taught completely in English. Most Hispanic parents of LEP children had their child enrolled in a bilingual program with at least some native tongue instruction.

Three-quarters of the parents of LEP children who preferred the bilingual program did so solely because they wanted to maintain their native language and culture. Fewer than one-quarter preferred the bilingual program because they believed it was the best and fastest way to learn English. Among all parents of LEP children, 36 percent preferred bilingual education over a regular classroom solely because they wanted to maintain their native language and culture. No trade-off question was asked, and so these results undoubtedly overestimate support.

CARDOZA, SANCHEZ, AND MENDOZA SURVEY

Before the 1988 ETS survey, the most extensive exploration of the attitudes of the language minority population was done in 1985 by Cardoza, Sanchez, and Mendoza, who surveyed a non-representative sample of about 200 adults from each of four language minority groups—two of them Hispanic and two of them Asian.[6] Because programs for LEP students were rated highly, Cardoza, Sanchez, and

Mendoza concluded that all groups were very favorably disposed toward bilingual education. However, we think their data, shown in table 7-1, actually show a general preference for any kind of help for language minority students, since there is not much difference in the perceived effectiveness of the three types of programs—TBE, ESL, and bilingual maintenance. Moreover, ESL programs, not bilingual education programs, generally receive the highest ratings.

These data also show less support on the part of Asian parents than Hispanic parents for any special program for language minority children. Although the Japanese are less supportive of any special program than the Chinese, the differences between Asians and Hispanics are greater than the differences within each group.[7]

Cardoza, Sanchez, and Mendoza also found that the more familiar the respondent was with bilingual education programs, the more favorably he or she rated the programs. Indeed, familiarity with the program was the major predictor of favorable attitudes in their regression analysis.

Table 7-1
Cardoza, Sanchez, and Mendoza 1985 Survey of Language Minority Adults

	Cuban	Mexican-American	Both Hispanic Groups	Chinese	Japan-ese	Both Asian Grps.
Mean perceived effectiveness of:	[Scale = 4 to 16]					
TBE	12.43	12.55	12.5	11.85	10.54	11.2
ESL	12.31	12.80	12.6	11.77	11.48	11.6
Maintenance	12.19	12.38	12.3	11.55	10.42	11.0
Mean preference for enrolling own child in:	[Scale = 0 to 3]					
TBE	2.32	2.22	2.3	2.03	1.63	1.8
ESL	2.46	2.44	2.4	2.24	1.68	1.9
Maintenance	2.42	2.16	2.3	1.83	1.36	1.6
Accept higher taxes to support:	[Scale 0 to 2]					
TBE	1.34	1.23	1.3	1.02	0.68	0.8
ESL	1.34	1.40	1.4	0.94	1.00	1.0
Maintenance	1.44	1.18	1.3	1.02	0.57	0.8

Source: D. Cardoza, A. Sanchez, and R. Mendoza, "Attitudes Toward Bilingual Education and Foreign Language Instruction Among Four Ethnolinguistic Groups," Los Alamitos, CA: National Center for Bilingual Research, 1985, tables 10-12.

Huddy and Sears

Huddy and Sears (1990) found just the opposite. Only 22 percent of the Huddy and Sears national sample of 1,170 non-Hispanic adults were able to give a roughly accurate description of bilingual education.[8] Almost 40 percent described it as bilingualism or foreign language instruction, and 29 percent were unable to give any description at all. Despite the fact that three-quarters of respondents could not accurately describe bilingual education, a majority supported bilingual education.

Hakuta Survey

In Hakuta's 1985 survey of 216 adults in New Haven (37 of them Spanish-speaking), 76 percent of the respondents agreed that the emphasis of bilingual education should be to encourage students to enter English-only classes as quickly as possible, yet 58 percent agreed that the emphasis should be on maintaining the Spanish language and culture of the children.[9] In other words, at least 34 percent[10] of the respondents thought that bilingual education should put the emphasis on *both* entering English-only classes as quickly as possible *and* on maintaining the Spanish language and culture of the children. It is clear that unless respondents are explicitly asked to consider the trade-off they will not. In this case they should have been asked whether they wanted to emphasize maintaining the Spanish language even if it meant that a student's entry into an English-only classroom would not occur quickly.

The 1988 ETS Survey

The ETS nationwide survey (Baratz-Snowden et al.) of 867 Asian, 904 Mexican-American, 631 Puerto Rican, and 502 Cuban language minority parents found some interesting differences in opinions on bilingual education between Asian and Hispanic parents and some equally fascinating inconsistencies in parental support for various options.[11]

THE SAMPLE

The survey sample was drawn from two sources. The first was a national sample of parents of Asian, Puerto Rican, and Mexican-American students in grades three, seven, and eleven. These students had participated in a special study of language minority students conducted as part of the National Assessment of Educational Progress (NAEP). For the 1986 NAEP, the U.S. Department of Education expanded the NAEP sample to cover language minority students so that additional analyses could be done on the school achievement of these students.

The second source was a supplementary telephone sample of Puerto Rican and Cuban parents of language minority elementary, middle, and high school students in New York and Miami. It was necessary to supplement the NAEP sample for Cuban parents because the refusal of the Dade County school system to release a list of the parents' names and addresses for NAEP-tested students decimated the NAEP Cuban sample. New York City required ETS to get the permission of the parents for interviews before interviewing them, and this decimated the Puerto Rican sample. In both cases, the NAEP sample was supplemented with a probability sample of the relevant ethnic group drawn from metropolitan area telephone lists.

Because there was no representative NAEP sample of Puerto Rican and Cuban parents, only the Mexican-American and Asian parents can be treated as representative samples. Although the Puerto Rican and Cuban samples provide some interesting additional information, they must be used with great caution.

Most of the analyses presented in this chapter are thus limited to the nationally representative samples of 867 Asian parents and 904 Mexican-American parents. It should be kept in mind that these are parents of language minority children, not necessarily parents of LEP children. Only a small percentage of the parents in the sample had children whom they and/or personnel in the school deemed to be so limited in English that they could not benefit from instruction in English.

Although the sample was of language minority parents rather than of the parents of LEP students, a sizable percentage, from one-third of Asians and Puerto Ricans to one-half of Mexican-Americans, spoke English poorly or not at all. Only one-third could speak it "very well." Thus, there was extensive use of the non-English language in the study sample—half or more of the Hispanic groups were administered the survey in Spanish at their request. Although most Asians were interviewed in English, family members and neighbors often assisted in translation.

THE SURVEY FINDINGS

The survey instrument covered areas relating to parents' attitudes toward school programs and practices; their aspirations for their children; their perceptions of their children's overall education, language learning, and language use; their level of involvement in their children's schooling; and also demographic characteristics. Baratz-Snowden et al. found that these language minority parents do not really understand bilingual education. As they pointed out "there was as much 'teaching' as there was gathering information concerning the three types of programs—bilingual, transitional, and immersion (p. 27)."

The first thing the ETS survey shows is that these language minority parents overwhelmingly want their children to learn English—

more than 97 percent of Mexican-American and Asian parents agree that it is *very* important that their children speak the English language well. On the other hand, 75 percent of Mexican-American and 53 percent of Asian parents also agree that it is *very* important that their children speak their native language well. On the surface then, language minority parents want it all (and in that respect are completely Americanized), although their number one priority is English.

Most of these parents do not think native language proficiency should be taught in school. As shown below, less than 30 percent of Mexican-American and Asian parents whose child does not speak or understand English very well think the child would be helped by instruction in the native tongue. Almost half of Mexican-American and 60 percent of Asian parents think that teaching in the native tongue interferes with learning English. Nevertheless, only 28 percent of Mexican-American and 67 percent of Asian parents prefer that reading and writing be taught only in English, and only 39 percent of Mexican-American and 68 percent of Asian parents prefer that basic subjects be taught only in English. The percentages preferring reading and writing and basic subjects be taught in both languages is shown in parentheses below those preferring only English. That means from 15 to 25 percent of Mexican-American parents believe *both* that learning in the native language interferes with English *and* that reading and writing and/or basic subjects should be taught partly in the native language.[12]

	Mexican-American	Asian
*[If child does not speak or understand English very well] would it help the child if classes were taught using the non-English language? (% yes)	29	28

% parents agreeing that teaching *in* non-English language interferes with learning English	43	60
% who prefer reading and writing be taught only in English *(in both languages)*	28 *(70)*	67 *(32)*
% who prefer basic subjects be taught only in English *(in both languages)*	39 *(56)*	68 *(30)*

Most language minority parents do not think the school should have the primary responsibility for teaching their child to *speak* the non-English language. Only 28 percent of Mexican-American and less than 10 percent of Asian parents believe this. A little less than half of Mexican-American parents, however, believe that the school has the primary responsibility to teach *literacy* in the native language, although only 10 percent of Asian parents think so. Support for a primary role for the schools drops significantly regarding ethnic studies—only 28 percent of Mexican-American and 16 percent of Asian parents think the school has the primary responsibility to teach ethnic studies.

	Mexican-American	Asian
% parents agreeing "the school has the primary responsibility to teach speaking the non-English language"	28	10
% parents agreeing "the school has the primary responsibility to teach literacy in the non-English language"	48	10
% parents agreeing "the school has the primary responsibility to teach ethnic heritage"	28	16

The question on native tongue instruction likely to produce the greatest support would be one in which the parent is *told* it is beneficial. In this case only 47 percent of Mexican-American parents think that language minority children should be taught math and science in the non-English language *even* if it means they would learn better. Even fewer Asian parents—23 percent—support native tongue instruction even if it means the language minority child would learn better.

	Mexican-American	Asian
Should math and science be taught in the non-English if it means language minority students will learn better? (% yes)	47	24

While a minority of parents support native tongue instruction even if told it helps language minority students and almost half believe it interferes with learning English, a fairly large percentage support programs for non-English speakers that have the word "bilingual" in them as well as those that have the phrase "all English." As shown below, 80 percent of Mexican-American parents and 55 percent of Asian parents support bilingual maintenance programs for non-English speakers. An even larger percentage—85 and 65 percent respectively—support transitional bilingual education programs. On the other hand, 67 percent of Mexican-American parents and 81 percent of Asian parents support *all English* immersion programs for non-English speaking children. In short, 52 percent of Mexican-American parents support *both* a transitional bilingual education program *and* an all English program. Almost as large a percentage—47 percent—support *both* a bilingual maintenance program *and* an all English program. More than 40 percent of the Asian parents support *both* TBE *and* all English programs, and 30 percent support *both* a bilingual maintenance *and* an all English program.

	Mexican-American	Asian
% of parents who say a bilingual maintenance program is good for non-English speakers	80	55
% of parents who say a TBE program is good for non-English speakers	85	65
% of parents who say an *all English* immersion program is good for non-English speakers	67	81

The source of the support for all of these programs, regardless of the type, probably stems from the fact that an overwhelming majority of parents think language minority children should get some kind of extra help, particularly in learning English, and they are not clear about differences between types of help. However, there are significant differences between Mexican-American and Asian parents on this issue. As shown below, 82 percent of Mexican-American, but only 64 percent of Asian parents, think such children need extra help in learning English. Fifty-nine percent of Mexican-American, but only 40 percent of Asian parents, think language minority children should get extra help learning other subjects at school—a 20 percentage point difference between the two groups.

	Mexican-American	Asian
% agreeing "language minority children should get extra help learning English at school"	82	64

% agreeing "language minority children should get extra help learning other subjects at school"	59	40

More than 81 percent of Mexican-American and 62 percent of Asian parents believe that the schools should teach *all* children, not just non-English-speaking children, a second language. Thus, some of the support for programs that mention the word "bilingual" may stem from support for foreign language instruction for all students as well as support for special programs that help language minority children.

When language minority parents were asked whether they would like their own child in a bilingual program, support for such programs dropped by 25 to 30 points. But so did support for all English programs. This phenomenon reinforces the idea that much of the support for "bilingual education" is support for extra help, which most of these parents did not think their child needed.

	Mexican-American	Asian
% of parents who would like their child to be in a bilingual maintenance program	56	25
% of parents who would like their child to be in a TBE program	52	25
% of parents who would like their child to be in an *all English* immersion program	45	44

Indeed, 87 percent of Mexican-American and 88 percent of Asian parents rated their child's English language ability as pretty good or very good.[13] When asked if any of their children attended classes outside school to learn their native language and culture, only 4 percent of Mexican-American and 22 percent of Asian parents replied affirmatively.

Another set of questions in the ETS survey does much to illuminate the extent of the confusion on the part of parents when they gave the above responses. When language minority parents were asked whether the schools should teach non-English-speaking children their native language if it means less time for teaching them other subjects, the support for teaching the non-English language dropped from 70 percent of Mexican-American parents to around 12 percent when it meant reducing time in academic subjects and to 22 percent when it meant reducing art and music. For Asian parents, it dropped from 32 percent to 11 percent when reducing academic subjects and to 16 percent when reducing art and music.[14] Explicitly asking the trade-off question shows how much failing to ask it overestimates support for programs that include native tongue instruction.

Table 7-2
Parental Support for Reducing Time in School Subjects in Order to Teach in Non-English Language

Do you think the schools should teach non-English language speaking children the non-English language if it means less time for teaching them (% yes)	Mexican-American	Asian
English	12	11
Math	11	11
Science	13	10
Art	21	16
Music	22	17

The ETS survey suggests that parents are conflicted about native tongue instruction and confused about bilingual education. The fact that it takes a direct question regarding the loss in time for other subjects that instruction in a non-English language produces suggests that the issue of bilingual education is just not that salient to language minority parents. This is borne out by a non-directive question that was asked of parents in the ETS survey.

Non-directive questions (those that do not directly ask about the topic of interest) are among the best methods of getting at a person's underlying attitude. With non-directive questions, the respondent reveals his or her feelings without being prompted by the question to address a certain topic. It is thought that such methods are more accurate in assessing how strongly the person really feels about something. For example, if we ask, "What do you like to do in your leisure time?," and the respondent mentions playing basketball, we can more confidently conclude that the respondent likes to play basketball than if we ask, "Do you like to play basketball?," and the respondent says "yes."

To take advantage of the power of indirect questions, the ETS interview began with some general questions and an indirect question about what the parents wanted from the schools before any questions specifically mentioning bilingual education or related topics were asked. Language minority parents were asked to name the three most important things they wanted their children to learn in school. In coding this question, any subject mentioned in a respondent's top three choices was counted equally, and the percentage of parents who mentioned a subject at least once was computed.

Table 7-3 shows both the percent of parents who named a subject and where that subject fell in the rank order of the 14 subjects coded in response to the question. For example, the most common reply—a general reference to academic subjects—was mentioned by 72 percent of the Mexican-American parents and 66 percent of the Asian parents, and it is ranked first in importance by both groups.

Ranked in second place is English. While English is also included in the more general category of academic subjects, parents clearly felt strongly enough about English to name it specifically as a desired goal. Compared to English, the non-English language is of low priority—ranked 7th for Mexican-American parents with only 10 percent mentioning it (5 percent of the Mexican-American parents also specifically mentioned both languages), and 10th for Asians with only 4 percent listing it among their top three educational goals for the school.

Educators continually stress that programs for language minority youth are bicultural as well as bilingual and that teaching ethnic heritage is a key part of the curriculum. We see in table 7-3 that there is, for all practical purposes, no desire on the part of either Mexican-American or Asian parents for the schools to teach ethnic heritage. While a minority—4 to 10 percent—of language minority parents see the non-English language as something that should be taught at school, very few of them see ethnic heritage as a topic of any importance.

Table 7-3
Academic Subjects Mentioned as Among the Three Most Important Things They Wanted Their Children to Learn at School

	% Mexican-American	Rank	% Asian	Rank
Academic subjects	72	1	66%	1
English	47	2	51	2
General education	25	3	25	3
Extra-curricula [art, sports]	9	8	16	4
Social skills	11	5	13	5
Discipline, good work habits	10	7*	10	6
Prepare for work/career	13	4	9	7
Study skills/attitudes	7	9	7	9*
Citizenship/acculturation	3	12*	7	9*
non-English language	10	7*	4	11
Prepare for college	3	12*	6	10
Religion, values	3	12*	3	12
Both languages	5	10	0	14
Ethnic heritage	0.6	14	0.7	13

* = ties in the rank order

CONCLUSION

These surveys show that bilingual education and native language instruction are of low salience for adults in general and for language minority parents. If bilingual education were a more salient issue, people would not only be able to describe it accurately but their opinions would not be so sensitive to the specific wording of the questions. Nor would we find a large minority of parents simultaneously supporting mutually exclusive positions.

The evidence that bilingual education and native language instruction are of low priority is not only inferred from the inconsistent responses of respondents, but from a non-directive question from the ETS survey. When asked to rank the three most important things they wanted their child to learn at school, teaching the non-English language came to the minds of only 4 to 10 percent of the parents, and almost no one mentioned ethnic heritage.

Other questions show the same thing. Almost 98 percent of language minority parents said that learning English was very important, and fewer than half the parents, including Mexican-American parents, thought that the school had the primary responsibility to teach literacy in the native language.

We think some of the support shown for bilingual education reflects general support for any special program for language minority children. This conclusion stems from the fact that although more parents surveyed support English language programs for LEP students than support native language programs for LEP students, the differences in support are not large. Support for bilingual education programs is undoubtedly inflated by the fact that parents do not completely understand what they are beyond the fact that they are special help programs for limited-English-proficient children.

One of the clearest findings of the surveys reviewed above is that support for native language instruction varies among specific language minority groups. On the whole, Asian parents are less supportive of these options than are Hispanic parents.[15]

Obviously, the trade-off issue is critical to obtaining accurate opinions on bilingual education—yet it has only been asked in one survey over the last 15 years. When parents are asked whether the schools should teach non-English-speaking children the non-English language *even* if it means less time for teaching them English, math, or science, support for bilingual education plummets. There is apparently no part of the regular school day that most parents are willing to give up in return for instruction in two languages. As bilingual education is currently practiced, it takes time from the regular school day. Therefore, as it is currently practiced it goes against the wishes of language minority parents.

CHAPTER EIGHT

WHAT WE HAVE FOUND AND WHAT MUST BE DONE

Bilingual education has come to mean many things to many people. Indeed, the lack of clarity in the use of the term is one of the many problems with evaluating programs. Throughout this book, we have tried to use the term only to mean a full-time program that includes instruction in the native language, unless we specifically qualified it with "nominal" or "apparent." It is only by being precise about the term that we can even begin to understand its effects. There are times, however, when we feel this is an impossible task. The January 7, 1996, *Boston Globe,* for example, contained a story about a suburban school district with the exclamation "bilingual education is in full swing..." Yet this particular school district has *all* its so-called TBE students in regular classrooms all day, and there is no native tongue instruction. The students have at most an hour of ESL instruction taught daily in English. We do not consider this bilingual education at all, but rather regular classroom instruction with ESL pullout.

We suspect the benefit of bilingual education has been exaggerated in the eyes of many by such imprecise terminology. Our research indicates there are three *very* different programs for LEP students—native tongue instruction transitioning to English, structured immersion, and regular classroom instruction with ESL pullout—all being implemented in Massachusetts and all being called transitional bilingual education by state and local administrators and educators. A perceived benefit from any one of these alternatives is credited to transitional bilingual education even though only the first alternative actually is TBE.

On the other hand, the harm of transitional bilingual education—that is, first learning to read and write in the native language and learning subject matter in the native language—is similarly exaggerated by the many critics who fail to distinguish between the characteristics students come to school with and the effects of the programs in which they are enrolled. Bilingual education programs are not a disaster compared to other approaches, and students do learn English in *the average program of native tongue instruction as currently practiced most of the time by most teachers*. If children do leave TBE programs not knowing how to read and write in English, as critics allege, there is a good chance that they have learning problems, beyond simply not knowing English, that would have delayed their progress in any instructional environment. In short, many critics of TBE engage in their own type of fuzzy thinking by failing to control for other factors when evaluating the outcome of TBE.

This does not mean TBE is a superior technique. It is quite clear that Massachusetts is unjustified in going way beyond the federal government and other states, in not only *requiring* a full-time program in which the child learns to read and write in the native language and in English, but in requiring it if there are 20 LEP students of a single language group in the district—the equivalent of only one to two students per grade.[1] Not only is there no rationale for this fiscally irresponsible figure, but at the time it was implemented in 1971 there was not even a pedagogical theory to justify this approach.

Only after a decade of bilingual education programs implemented all over the United States and Massachusetts, with evaluations that showed inconsistent results, did Jim Cummins come up with a pedagogical theory—the facilitation theory—to justify a policy that had been implemented initially on civil rights grounds. The conflicting research on TBE was accounted for by whether or not the mysterious native tongue threshold had been reached by the students. Many teachers in Massachusetts' bilingual education programs believe in this theory, taught in their bilingual certification courses, because they have observed phenomena that seem to support it. First, over the years they have noticed that older immigrant students who were literate in their native language had an easier time learning English than did younger students who were not literate in their native language. In addition, they have observed that older students who were literate in their native language had an easier time learning English than students of the same age who were not literate in their native language. Some teachers who have taught night school have observed the same phenomenon—adults who were literate in their native language learned English faster than adults who were not literate in their native language.

These teachers might have figured out on their own that the true causal variable in each of these instances was not literacy in the native language but the age of the student (older students learn faster than younger students) or the presence of learning disabilities in older, illiterate students or an impoverished home life that prevented an older individual from becoming literate. They might even have realized that whatever benefit there is from being literate in one's native language is offset by the time it takes to acquire that literacy if that is not one's ultimate goal. But most of them were able to ignore these causal factors and alternative remedies because they were at the same time getting emphatic messages from intellectuals that children *must* become literate in their native language before they can reach the greatest level of proficiency in the second language. In this environment, it was and is easy to interpret one's own experience as confirming the theory and to ignore other possible explanations and remedies.

The TBE teachers most likely to believe that becoming literate in one's native language is necessary for the full development of one's cognitive abilities and ultimately for achievement in English are the Spanish TBE teachers. A number of factors make it easy for them to believe in the facilitation theory—there are often enough Spanish-speaking LEP students to fill a classroom; there are numerous certified teachers who are fluent in Spanish, including many non-native speakers; Spanish and English both use the Roman alphabet, and thus the transfer of skills seems more likely. Because is it *possible* for Spanish TBE teachers to teach according to the theory, they tend to accept it as generally valid and superior.

Similarly, because it is often not even possible for the non-Spanish TBE teachers to teach according to the facilitation theory—either the language does not use the Roman alphabet or it is not the official language of a large country and/or has numerous dialects or there are no published materials in the language—they tend not to believe in it. Some of them believe instead in the "self-esteem" theory of second language learning since this is the one thing they think they can do—improve their students' self-esteem by providing a protective learning environment and a positive role model. Others may simply believe that their students need a protected environment while they are learning English so that English can be taught at a pace and at a level the students can understand. And some of these teachers believe their students do just fine in a regular classroom environment with some ESL support.

Perhaps one of the more serious flaws of the facilitation theory is its lack of attention to non-Roman or non-alphabetic languages that have no similarity to English in appearance and take much longer to master. Learning to read in the native language may actually be harder in these languages than in the second language, if the latter is English or another Roman alphabet language. As a result, we know of no bilingual education programs in the United States that actually teach initial literacy in a non-alphabetic native language, although many programs may appear to—they are taught in self-contained classrooms, are called bilingual education, and receive bilingual education funding. We also do not know of any non-Roman alphabet bilingual education programs, even if the alphabet is phonetic (e.g., Hebrew, Arabic, the Indian dialects, Russian, and Khmer), that teach initial literacy in the native language. We suspect this is because educators believe that it is too difficult or distracting to teach literacy in a language with a completely different alphabet. Some of these dialects have more than one alphabet, and there are rules regarding the combination of consonants and implied or missing vowels that are different from English and other Roman alphabet languages so that teaching such languages in an already packed to overflowing day is too formidable a task.

Thus, it is only the Spanish TBE programs that are taught according to the theory and, in general, only the Spanish TBE teachers who seem to be knowledgeable about the theory and believe in it. The non-Spanish "TBE" teachers tend not to believe in the theory and do not teach according to it because it is not practical for them to do so.

The Effectiveness of Transitional Bilingual Education

Unfortunately there has been no scientific research conducted in Massachusetts evaluating the TBE programs that have been in place over the last 25 years. There has been some scientific research, however, conducted in other states and countries over this period. As discussed in chapter 3, Rossell and Baker (1996) reviewed hundreds of studies conducted from the 1960s to the present. Of 300 program evaluations we were able to locate, only 72 conformed to the standards for a scientific study. While we cannot be sure what was going on in these classrooms, there is a good possibility that the programs classified as TBE did include at least some native tongue instruction because, with only a few exceptions, they were for Spanish speakers. There is also a possibility that in some, and perhaps many, of the programs for Spanish speakers the native tongue instruction was minimal. Our observation of bilingual education programs over the last two decades is that there are very few bilingual maintenance programs—most programs transition students completely to English within three years even though they may remain in so-called bilingual education classrooms. Thus, the bias introduced by our not knowing exactly how much native tongue instruction was used is probably to overestimate its use in TBE programs and to overestimate as well the positive effect of TBE on academic achievement in English.

With these caveats, our findings are that the harm of transitional bilingual education as it is *currently practiced* has been exaggerated in comparison to the alternative typically practiced in American schools—regular classroom instruction with ESL pullout—since about half the time it does no worse than the latter in reading and math achievement. On the other hand, there is no evidence that TBE is a superior instructional technique, either. One-third of the studies found TBE to be worse than doing nothing in math and reading achievement, and two-thirds found it worse than doing nothing in language achievement.

There is one program for special language instruction—structured immersion—that is almost always superior to TBE. Structured immersion has many of the positive characteristics of transitional bilingual education. It provides a protected environment, but without the native tongue instruction. LEP children are in a self-contained classroom with a teacher trained in second language acquisition techniques who, in theory, teaches at a speed they can understand because supposedly everyone in the classroom is at the same level of comprehension. Of course, in U.S. classrooms, it is rare for everyone to be at the same level, regardless of the instructional technique being used, because children arrive from foreign countries not knowing a word of English every day of the school year including the last one.

The major, and most recent, evaluation of transitional bilingual education compared to structured immersion was the Ramirez et al. (1991) study. While there are enough problems with this study that it should be interpreted with great caution,[2] the fact that the early-exit (TBE) program did as well as it did in comparison to structured immersion suggests the following possibility: bilingual education may be superior to all English instruction in the very beginning when a student literally knows no English, but as the student's English language knowledge increases and English becomes more comprehensible, time on task in English becomes more important because it becomes *effective* time on task. Thus there is no difference between the effects of these two types of programs if the TBE students are transitioned fairly quickly to English.

Ramirez et al. (1991), on the other hand, shows *no* support for the facilitation theory since in that study the students who stayed in bilingual education the longest did the worst. While this apparently negative finding for bilingual education may not be valid given the lack of statistical control for student and classroom characteristics, it is definitively *not* positive evidence.

This and other research suggest that a little bit of native tongue instruction is not harmful and may even help LEP children when they literally know no English. Once students have some understanding of English, however, the reduced time on task in English in the TBE programs becomes a real detriment to their achievement. We suspect that this occurs sometime during the first year.

THE IMPLEMENTATION OF BILINGUAL EDUCATION PROGRAMS IN MASSACHUSETTS

The Massachusetts Transitional Bilingual Education Act, Chapter 71A, by requiring a full-time TBE program when there are only 20 LEP students of a single language group in a district, is wholly unrealistic. It is remarkable that this criterion has been allowed to stay in the legislation for 25 years since there is no school district in Massachusetts that has the resources to operate full-time programs of native tongue instruction with 1 or 2 students in a classroom (or 2 to 4 in a classroom if two grades are combined) taught by a $39,000-a-year teacher fluent in the children's native language. It is even more remarkable that this threshold is allowed to exist when we consider the fact that there are 20 or more LEP students from each of the following language groups in one or more districts in Massachusetts: Spanish, "Chinese" (Cantonese?, Mandarin?), Khmer, Portuguese, Cape Verdean (which dialects?), Greek, Italian, Arabic, Armenian, Haitian Creole (which dialects?), Laotian, Russian, Vietnamese, Hmong, Hebrew, Japanese, Korean, Polish, and Gujarati. Even if school districts could afford classes of 1 to 4 students, there are not enough teachers qualified to teach in each of these languages and English.

Strangely, almost everyone seems to know the law is unrealistic, and yet no one wants to challenge it. To do so is to invite public scrutiny and hostility. Moreover, almost no one believes the outcome of such a challenge will be a more realistic law. The most common, obviously cynical, prediction is that the state will be pressured by TBE advocacy groups to compel school districts into compliance with the law, not that the law will be changed so that it can be realistically enforced. So everyone—from state bureaucrats to local school district administrators—pretends that the law makes sense and that it is being obeyed.

How Long Should a Child Stay in "Bilingual Education?"

Perhaps one of the greatest obstacles to effective implementation in this field is the complexity of the logic regarding the policy. As a result of this complexity, the answers to the following critical questions in bilingual education are often confused: First, how long does it take for a LEP child to master enough English so that the regular classroom is a positive learning experience? Second, when do LEP students no longer need special help? Third, how long does it take LEP students to become completely fluent in English?

The literature on bilingual education is confused on these issues, thanks in large part to the writings of Jim Cummins and his distinction between everyday communications skills and academic proficiency. Many educators and administrators have interpreted the one empirical study he conducted and its finding that it takes five to seven years to master the second language to the level of academic proficiency as the answer to all three questions. It is not; these are separate questions with separate answers, and Cummins' research is only even relevant to the second question—when does a child no longer need special help?

To the first question, we suspect that *it is probably a matter of months before a child can benefit from a regular English classroom.* It cannot be emphasized enough that although TBE is supposed to be a remedy for an apparently discredited and presumptively unconstitutional technique—regular classroom enrollment—the argument for TBE fails on both logic and empirical grounds. The triggering point for TBE in Massachusetts is 20 students of a single language group in a district. Does this mean that LEP children who number fewer than 20 do just fine? If something is a discredited approach and a violation of a child's civil rights, it is so whether there is one child or 1,000 children. Of the nearly 40,000 LEP students in the state, only 57 percent (the Spanish speakers) are even potentially receiving native tongue instruction according to the theory and the law—that is, taught to read and write in their native language. Based on our observations, another 8,000 or so students—about 20 percent of the LEP students—are in structured immersion classes that are mislabeled bilingual education. The rest are in regular classrooms with ESL pullout. Thus, a majority of LEP children in Massachusetts are receiving all-English instruction and appear to be doing fine.

The second question is, when do LEP students no longer need special help? The answer is that *the need for special help varies greatly from child to child.* For any particular child, it could be many years—Cummins' research suggests an average of five to seven years. For some children, however, it could be a few months. Indeed, the current limit of three years for "bilingual education" may be too short for many students if by 'bilingual education' we mean special help. Children who are not fluent in English and older children who are not literate in their native language clearly need special help, and they may need it for many, many years. Thus, while there is no evidence that these children need to become literate in their native language, simple logic suggests they probably need help beyond what the regular classroom teacher can provide, and a three-year time limit is an arbitrary constraint with no research justification.

The final question is, how long does it take a LEP student to become completely fluent in English? The answer is that *it may take decades for a child to become fully proficient in English,* just as it may for some native English speakers. But that has nothing to do with whether such children must be taught in their native language or even in a self-contained classroom. If we waited for children to be fully proficient in English before we allowed them into a regular classroom, many English monolingual students would never be allowed in!

The failure to understand that these three questions and their answers are distinct and separate helps perpetuate the confusion surrounding bilingual education policy.

Lowering the Heat on the Policy Debate

Before making any policy recommendations, we would like to urge that the policy debate be civilized by acknowledging that most bilingual education teachers—those who teach their students to read and write in their native language and teach them subject matter in their native language—and the people who support bilingual education so defined are generally competent professionals who have only the best intentions. They sincerely believe that native language literacy and instruction in the native language help their students. In fact, the harm from TBE as it is generally practiced is *not* serious for most students when compared to the regular classroom. Indeed, we should have expected this. American teachers, including bilingual education teachers, would not be implementing a practice year after year if they believed that it harmed children.

In general, the teachers who believe native tongue instruction *is* harmful simply subvert the policy rather than directly challenging it. All over Massachusetts (and the United States), Chinese, Greek, Portuguese, Cape Verdean, Haitian, Vietnamese, Cambodian, and other non-Spanish-speaking LEP students, are being taught to read and write in English and taught content area in English in self-contained classrooms of LEP children of the same language group in programs mislabeled bilingual education. Even in the Spanish TBE classrooms, many teachers either teach the children to read and write in English only, or transition them so rapidly from Spanish to English reading and writing that there appears to be little or no harm done by native tongue instruction. If we include these programs under the umbrella of "bilingual education" along with true bilingual education programs (those that really do teach literacy in the native language), it is not hard to see why TBE has so many supporters. In its most harmful form TBE is only practiced for Spanish speakers and even then only for some unknown percentage of them.

This is not to say there are no bad apples teaching or supporting TBE—that is, individuals who are more concerned with maintaining the status quo and their careers than they are with the effects of TBE on children. Some Spanish TBE teachers and advocates undoubtedly believe in, and teach according to, the facilitation theory because it is in their self-interest to do so. Spanish bilingual programs represent a lot of jobs for teachers, psychologists, and administrators. It is easy for we human beings to convince ourselves that a program that benefits us is also a worthwhile program for the individuals it is supposed to benefit. This process of self-persuasion is made easier by the fact that there are so many intellectuals who derive no direct benefit from the program who are telling TBE teachers what many want to hear—that the only way for children to avoid a cognitive deficit is for them to be literate in their native language. It is also made easier by the symbolic ethnic politics surrounding this issue. To be pro-"bilingual education" is to be pro-Hispanic or pro-immigrant. To be anti-"bilingual education" is to be anti-Hispanic or anti-immigrant. Nevertheless, we categorically reject the allegation that but a handful of TBE teachers and administrators cynically use a technique they think harms children in order to stay employed and to keep their friends employed.

By the same token, critics of bilingual education also have a reasonable position since the theory behind bilingual education is counterintuitive and contrary to all other educational theory.[3] In addition, just because TBE is not a uniform disaster in practice does not mean it isn't detrimental to any individual student. The theory underlying

TBE if actually followed could produce large numbers of Spanish-speaking students who spend their entire educational careers trying to become fully proficient in Spanish before transitioning to English. Good policy should be based on sound theory and logic; it should not depend on the common sense of those who implement it to subvert or change it.

Policy Recommendations

1) Free School Districts from the Legal Obligation to Provide Native Tongue Instruction.

The first and most important policy recommendation is that school districts should be freed from the legal obligation to provide programs in native tongue instruction to LEP children. This is different from prohibiting native tongue instruction. The political reality is that native tongue instruction has too many supporters to be abolished any time soon even if there were overwhelming evidence that it is harmful. This being the case, the recommendations that follow are designed to minimize any harmful effect of native tongue instruction.

- Throughout Chapter 71A, the term *educational programs for limited-English-proficient children* (or some other neutral phrase) should be substituted for transitional bilingual education.
- In addition, the term "teacher of transitional bilingual education" should be changed throughout Chapter 71A to a more neutral term such as "teacher of educational programs for limited-English-proficient children."

2) Increase the LEP Population Size Needed to Trigger a Self-Contained Classroom.

The law should be changed so that districts are not required to offer a self-contained classroom, regardless of the language of instruction, until the number of LEP students in any given *school* is at least 18 students in any particular *grade*. Even then they do not need to be of the same language group since they can be taught in an all-English, structured immersion program. One to two students per classroom is fiscally absurd, so is three, so is four, and so is eight, which would mean combining *four* grades. Nor should students be bused forcibly out of their neighborhood school or otherwise denied their school of choice in order to fill a LEP classroom unless and until it has been demonstrated by valid scientific research that they are better off in a central location being taught in a protected environment than they are in their neighborhood school. In any case, the district should not be obligated to keep a student in such a separate environment for more than one school year.

3) Require Parental Consent for Enrollment in a Self-Contained Classroom.

Chapter 71A, as currently written, first places the child identified as LEP in transitional bilingual education and then allows parents to withdraw the child by written notice to the school authorities, thus putting the burden on parents to disagree with the authorities and to disrupt their child's education. We think the burden should be on the school district. Parents should have to give their written consent *before* their child is enrolled in *any* program with a self-contained classroom of LEP students, regardless of the language of instruction.

4) Require English Language Fluency for Teachers in an Educational Program for LEP Children.

Teachers in educational programs for LEP children should not be granted certificates to teach LEP children unless they possess a bachelor's degree or better from an accredited university in the United States and meet the requirements set by the board for certification in second language acquisition teaching skills. If the teacher is not a graduate of an academic institution in the United States, he or she should be required to demonstrate fluency in written and spoken English by means of an examination, both oral and written.

The requirement for native tongue fluency is unnecessary since LEP children can be taught in an all-English, self-contained classroom of LEP students. In addition, research indicates that it is more important that a teacher be fully proficient in English than in the second language *if* one's goal is English language proficiency.[4]

In our classroom observations, we found a few teachers whose English skills were obviously and clearly inadequate. As a result, they taught entirely in Spanish. The current law (section 6) allows this to happen by requiring only "communicative skills in English" but demanding "a speaking and reading ability in a language other than English."

5) Change the Criteria for Entering and Exiting a Self-Contained Classroom.

A home language survey should identify students who are possibly limited English proficient by asking what language is most often spoken by the student. If it is a language other than English, this student should be referred to the Language Appraisal Team for each school or school district. This team should consist of administrators, regular classroom teachers, and teachers of limited-English-proficient children in self-contained classrooms (if they exist in the school). The Language Appraisal Team should also make the decision as to whether a child is ready to be mainstreamed. The classroom teacher's evaluation should be the major factor, not test scores, since teachers are better judges of the ability of students to survive in a regular English language classroom and better able to determine whether students need extra help than are tests of any kind. Except in unusual circumstances, a child should not be in a self-contained classroom for more than a year.

The annual census of the number of children of limited English-speaking ability and their primary languages (required of each school district in Massachusetts by Chapter 71A) should be based on the identification of students by the Language Appraisal Team.

6) Keep Class Sizes Small.

The class size for self-contained classrooms of LEP students, regardless of the language of instruction, probably should be smaller than that for regular classrooms. Nevertheless, the current limit of 18 students per class (assuming one teacher, without an aide) is somewhat arbitrary and not grounded in research on what is desirable for LEP children. Smaller class sizes would help boost achievement (see Glass et al., 1982) and help deal with the problem of children coming in throughout the school year and thus being at different stages of English language development. LEP students in regular classrooms should have ESL pullout or in-class, small group English language instruction on a daily basis.

Smaller class size does not have to be achieved by reducing the number of students in a classroom. It can also be achieved by increasing the number of instructors. This can be accomplished relatively inexpensively through peer tutoring by fluent English-speaking students, paraprofessional tutoring, and the use of other tutors who provide individualized instruction.

THE IDEAL PROGRAM

What scientific evidence there is on the effectiveness of alternative instructional programs for LEP children suggests that the best, and most cost-effective, program for LEP children is structured immersion. Such programs are implemented all over Massachusetts for *non-*

Spanish-speaking LEP students—Chinese, Cape Verdeans, Haitians, Vietnamese, Portuguese, etc.—under the label "transitional bilingual education." The language of instruction in a structured immersion program is English at a level the child can understand in a self-contained classroom of LEP students who are at approximately the same level of English language knowledge and the same age. The children in a structured immersion classroom do not have to be of the same language background, but the teacher should be trained in second language acquisition techniques. These programs should be fully integrated into regular schools so that students are exposed to English speakers on the playground, in the cafeterias, the halls, assemblies, and other areas before, during, and after school. Students should probably not remain in self-contained, second language acquisition classrooms for more than a year, even if the language of instruction is English. Another way of dealing with the problem of instructing LEP children at different stages of English language development is to extend the day for those who are behind. This might be a self-supporting program involving paraprofessional tutoring in English and a fee charged on a sliding scale. The general rule is that LEP students who are behind their classmates need more English language instruction on an individualized basis than Chapter 71A requires, not the same or less. If a student has a learning disability that prevents transition to a regular classroom within a year, he or she would in most cases probably be better off undergoing diagnostic testing and being referred to a more appropriate program.

Better Research

This ideal program is still relatively crude in a programmatic sense and could be refined further if there were better research. Such research could be done right here in Massachusetts. Chapter 71A as it is actually implemented is a natural laboratory for educational research comparing alternative instructional programs. The Commonwealth of Massachusetts should require local school districts to keep the kind of data that would allow social scientists to analyze variations in programs and the effects of these variations. The federal and state governments must fund more high-quality research by enlisting the aid of nationally respected social scientists in designing RFPs (Requests for Proposals) and evaluating proposals. The quality of research in this field is a national disgrace, which we do not think would be allowed if the subject were national defense or the economy. Assuming that the goal of bilingual education in the United States is to make LEP students successful in English and in an English language environment, we suggest several hypotheses to be tested by research:

1) Regarding TBE

   a) Native tongue instruction should be minimal and if used at all only in the beginning when a LEP student's English language knowledge is very low.

   b) The time period for the superiority of or need for native tongue instruction may be a matter of *months.*

   c) Teachers who are familiar with, but not fluent in, the child's native language are better teachers of LEP students than fluent speakers because the former will emphasize transition to English, and the latter will emphasize maintenance of the native tongue and development of the native tongue language arts, which ultimately will work to the detriment of academic achievement in English.

2) Regarding Structured Immersion

   a) Enrollment in a self-contained classroom should be no longer than a year.

   b) Students of the same language group should not be placed in the same classroom, if at all possible, as this will delay their English language development.

c) Teachers should not use the student's native language for instruction.

If these are accepted as viable hypotheses, researchers would have to design very different research studies from the ones we have seen in the past. A research study to test these hypotheses would look something like this:

> Treatment Groups: Truly LEP[5] students in classrooms categorized not by nominal program type but by the amount of English language instruction by subject matter and the varying credentials and native language ability of the teachers and aides.
>
> Covariates: Student background characteristics, including use of English at home and neighborhood, intelligence (nonverbal such as Raven's Progressive Matrices), and prior English language ability level and program.
>
> Outcome variables: Academic achievement by subject matter (as well as attitudes, drop out rates, etc.) measured every *three months* during the academic year, not simply at the beginning and end of the year.

It is important that outcome variables be measured in *months,* not years, because the purpose of this research is to delineate the time period during which a child is better off in a self-contained classroom and/or when native tongue instruction might be helpful.

The best study would involve *random* assignment to alternative language instruction programs, thus eliminating the need for a pretest—one of the banes of research in this field. A quasi-experimental design, in which the above covariates are used to make the different students in the two different treatments "equal," is, of course, a satisfactory alternative to random assignment or we would not have been able to do the literature review discussed in chapter 3. But in a policy area such as this, where sentiments run deep even among social scientists, convincing individuals on either side of the debate that the results of a study are to be taken seriously is easier with random assignment—the ideal form of scientific study—than it is with a quasi-experimental design. With random assignment one never has to worry about whether one has controlled for all the relevant variables.

It cannot be emphasized enough, however, that existing research clearly shows, as with all other educational interventions, that the intervention itself is the least important factor explaining achievement. The most important factors in a child's acquisition of English and other subjects are the child's family characteristics, his or her intelligence, the characteristics of his or her classmates, and the intelligence and talent of their teacher. For most students, at least in an educational system in which all programs provide substantial amounts of English, the exact percentage of each language has, on average, explained only a small portion of the variance in achievement.[6] Even in the worst cases we are struck by how small the difference in academic achievement is—a maximum of about 15 points on a norm-referenced standarized achievement test—between programs with very different amounts of English instruction. Nevertheless, averages can obscure the fact that for any single student there could be serious consequences to native tongue instruction according to the theory.

BILINGUAL MAINTENANCE AND TWO-WAY PROGRAMS

Since being bilingual is useful and Hispanic intellectuals and leaders are concerned about losing the Spanish language, that concern ought to be respected—particularly since English is no danger whatsoever of losing its status as our common (although not official) language.[7] We suggest this, not only so that school districts can avoid being labeled anti-immigrant or anti-Hispanic if they eliminate TBE but also because we believe that parents ought to have, within reason, the public schools they want.

If there is demand for it, native tongue instruction could be offered after school as a voluntary enrichment to the regular elementary school instructional day (the only kind of native tongue instruction program a majority of language minority parents want) on a sliding fee basis. The goal of these programs would be to teach literacy in Spanish (or another language), not because it is the best way to learn English and other subjects in which students will be tested in English—there is absolutely no evidence for that—but because it is a good way to learn Spanish while not suffering a deficit in English. We think it makes good politics and good pedagogy to enrich the curriculum of our schools by adding voluntary language instruction in Spanish and/or any other foreign language for which there is a demand.

We would advise, however, against attempts to wedge these bilingual maintenance programs into the regular school day, even if they are voluntary as with the two-way programs discussed below. Policymakers must consider three critical elements of consumer protection if they are to protect adequately the rights of LEP children. First, not all LEP children will want to, or be able to, maintain their native language. They should not be forced to do so. Second, children and their parents should be advised as to the probable consequences of being taught bilingually within the constraints of the normal school day. There is a strong chance they will fall behind in both languages. Third, policymakers should keep in mind that opinion surveys indicate that language minority parents overwhelmingly reject native tongue instruction during the regular school day.

Two-way bilingual education programs, classrooms consisting of English speakers and non-English speakers, are another choice that should be offered where there is demand. But as they are currently practiced within the confines of a normal school day, two-way bilingual education programs afford students less English language time than they would receive in an all English classroom and less non-

English language time than they would receive in a classroom composed of speakers of that language with instruction only in that language. As a result, their outcomes are rather mixed.[8] Thus, these programs should also be extended day in order to maximize the benefits of learning a second language and minimize the cost to learning English.

CONCLUSION: BAD THEORY SAVED BY GOOD PRACTICE

There are many academics who support bilingual education who believe that the reason it is not more successful is that it is not being implemented by educators according to the theory. We believe the opposite. The theory—that children must attain full proficiency in their native language before they transition to English—is unsubstantiated, and the evidence that exists suggests it is wrong. Thus, we believe, it is only the good sense and intelligence of many TBE teachers and administrators that have kept the program from being a total disaster. As it is currently practiced, TBE teachers do transition LEP students to English fairly quickly, even though the students may continue to be enrolled in the program, and it is this emphasis in most classrooms most of the time on transitioning to English that keeps the program viable.

However, a policy that depends on the good sense of the implementors to subvert it entirely (the non-Spanish TBE programs) or modify it so that it is not harmful (the very early transition Spanish TBE programs) is a policy that badly needs reform. We would like to see Chapter 71A, and the regulations that implement it, acknowledge that TBE can have serious risks because there is the occasional teacher who believes the pedagogical theory he or she has been taught and follows it to the letter.

If school districts want to implement TBE, parents should be aware of these risks before they enroll their children. Afterwards may be too late. In Los Angeles and Brooklyn, New York, Hispanic parents have recently brought court suits (the Brooklyn suit was dismissed without a hearing)[9] against their school districts, alleging that their children are being placed in Spanish language classrooms because of their surnames, that they never learn English adequately, and that they never get out of the program. This is the unfortunate risk of TBE, and even if it happens only some of the time, it is why, despite the good intentions of most of the professionals and intellectuals who support and practice it, we cannot recommend it as a program of compensatory education for limited-English-proficient children. The evidence at hand supports structured immersion—all English instruction in a self-contained classroom.

Notes

Chapter One: Introduction and Summary

[1] The Bilingual Education Commission, which prepared *Striving for Success: The Education of Bilingual Pupils,* December 1994, for the Massachusetts legislature, offers the following as a working definition of bilingual education: "...an educational program that uses two languages for instruction, English and another language. All bilingual programs are first and foremost intended to provide pupils with effective access to a full, high quality education. Currently, guidelines published by the Department of Education list a number of models of bilingual education options available for implementation in the Commonwealth....All models of bilingual education include an English as a Second Language (ESL) component" (p. 9). The term "bilingual education," however is commonly used in a generic or global sense to refer to any program that addresses the needs of language minority students, whether or not two languages are used. In this book we use the phrase bilingual education primarily in its strict sense—to refer to programs with a native language component. We use the qualifiers "nominal" or "apparent" when it is not known whether the program includes native language instruction or it is likely that it does not.

[2] See, for example, "Bilingual Education Evaluation," El Paso Independent School District, El Paso, TX, 1992.

[3] The Bilingual Education Commission offers the following working definition for transitional bilingual education: "...(TBE) is a model used by the vast majority of bilingual education programs in the Commonwealth and was established by M.G.L. Chapter 71A...TBE assists pupils in learning academic content through instruction in their native language, while simultaneously learning English as a Second Language. Typically, content instruction in English increases gradually until pupils have sufficient command of the language to be mainstreamed into English only classrooms" (p. 9).

[4] The Bilingual Education Commission lists six models of bilingual education in appendix B of *Striving for Success.* The bilingual maintenance program "...provides pupils whose first language is other than English with continued development and enrichment in their native language throughout their school experience" (p. 69).

[5] The term "Hispanic" was coined as a means of forming a political alliance within the United States of diverse ethnic groups with roots in countries where Spanish is spoken. The term has become widely used as

though it did in fact denote a single ethnic identity. In the literature on bilingual education, it is used to refer to students whose ancestors spoke Spanish whether or not the students themselves do. In different parts of the country, the ethnicity of Hispanics will differ significantly: in the West more Hispanics are of Mexican ancestry, in the Northeast of Puerto Rican, and in the Southeast of Cuban, etc.

[6] Masahito Okada et al., *Synthesis of Reported Evaluation and Research Evidence on the Effectiveness of Bilingual Education Basic Projects,* Los Alamitos, CA: National Center for Bilingual Research, 1983.

[7] American Legislative Exchange Council (ALEC) and U.S. English Foundation, *Bilingual Education in the United States 1991-92, Special Supplement, The Report Card on American Education 1994,* Washington, D.C., 1994.

[8] Bilingual Education Commission, *Striving for Success: The Education of Bilingual Pupils,* 41.

[9] Christine H. Rossell and Keith Baker, "The Educational Effectiveness of Bilingual Education," *Research in the Teaching of English* (February 1996), 30(1): 7-74.

CHAPTER TWO: THE LEGISLATIVE AND POLITICAL HISTORY OF BILINGUAL EDUCATION

[1] James F. Crawford, *Bilingual Education: History, Politics, Theory, and Practice*, Trenton, N.J.: Crane Publishing Company, 1989; Arnold H. Leibowitz, *Educational Policy and Political Acceptance: the Imposition of English as the Language of Instruction in American Schools*, Washington, D.C: National Clearinghouse for Bilingual Education, 1971.

[2] Crawford, 1989.

[3] Susan Kuyper, "The Americanization of German Immigrants: Language, Religion and Schools in Nineteenth Century Rural Wisconsin," Ph.D. dissertation, University of Wisconsin, 1980, cited in Steven L. Schlossman, "Is There an American Tradition of Bilingual Education? German in the Public Elementary Schools, 1840-1919," *American Journal of Education* (February 1983) 91: 144.

[4] National Center for Education Statistics, *The Condition of Education*, Washington, D.C.: U.S. Government Printing Office, 1992: 62.

[5] The Office of Bilingual Education and Minority Language Affairs (OBEMLA) has undergone several changes since it was first established as the Office of Bilingual Education in 1974.

[6] Rachel F. Moran, "Of Democracy, Devaluation, and Bilingual Education," *Creighton Law Review* (1993), 26: 255-319.

[7] See Christine Rossell and J. Michael Ross, "The social science evidence on bilingual education," *Journal of Law and Education* (1986), 15: 385-419.

[8] Keith Baker and Adriana de Kanter, *The effectiveness of bilingual education programs: A review of the literature, Final draft report*, Washington, DC: U.S. Department of Education, 1981.

[9] Massachusetts was followed by Alaska and California (1972); Arizona, Illinois, New Mexico, and Texas (1973); Michigan, New York, and Rhode Island (1974); Colorado, Louisiana, New Jersey, and Wisconsin (1975); Indiana (1976); Connecticut, Maine, Minnesota, and Utah (1977); and Iowa, Kansas, Oregon, and Washington (1979), according to Crawford, 1989: 49, fn. 4.

[10] It should be noted that when the base is 25 to 29 years old, as it was for the national data, this produces a 10- to 15-point higher percentage completing high school for whites and blacks than when the base is 25 years and older (figure 2-1) because the latter group includes older people who, because of historical patterns, are less likely to have completed high school.

[11] Richard M. Hailer, *Meeting the Needs of the Bilingual Child, A Historical Perspective of the Nation's First Transitional Bilingual Education Law: Chapter 71A of the Acts of 1971*, Commonwealth of Massachusetts, Boston: Massachusetts State Department of Education, Bureau of Transitional Bilingual Education, 1976.

[12] The council consisted of Alex Rodriguez (Assistant Executive Vice President, United Community Planning, Boston); Francesco Benenati (Director, Title VII, E.S.E.A., Lawrence Public Schools); Dr. Lawrence Brown (Director, Massachusetts Advocacy Center, Boston); Janet Bryant (Education Director, Massachusetts Commission Against Discrimination, Boston); Dr. Juan P. Caban (Assistant Professor, School of Education, Media Center, University of Massachusetts, Amherst); Ruben Cabral (Director, Cambridge Organized Portuguese Americans, Inc. (C.O.P.A.), Boston); John Corcoran (Coordinator, Bilingual Education Program, Worcester Public Schools); John R. Correiro (Director, Title VII, E.S.E.A., Fall River Public Schools); Raffael C. DeGruttola (Director, Title VII, E.S.E.A., Arts and Humanities Component, Mayor's Office of Cultural Affairs, Boston); Joseph Fernandez (Director, Bilingual Education, Cambridge Public Schools); Abel D. Fidaigo (Director, Title VII, E.S.E.A., New Bedford Public Schools); Frida Garcia (Special Assistant to the Governor on Spanish-speaking Affairs, State House, Boston); Dr. Argelia M. Buitrago Hermenet (Director, Bilingual Programs, Springfield Technical Community College); Judith Kennedy (Assistant Principal, Carew Street School, Springfield); Sister Lilian Lamoreux (Director of Education, Community of Gray Nuns, Lowell); John T. Mahoney (Federal Project Co-

ordinator, Holyoke Public Schools); Ignacia B. Mallon (Bilingual Program Coordinator, Framingham Public Schools); Armando Martinez (Director, Puente, Inc., Boston); Alice G. Meisel (Director, Title VII, E.S.E.A., Holyoke Public Schools); Adeline Naiman (Assistant to President, Education Development Center, Newton); Carmen C. Necheles (Acting Director, Department of Bilingual Education, Boston Public Schools); Dr. Richard Newman (Chairman, Department of Foreign Languages, Boston State College); Rev. Federico O'Brien (Spanish Apostolate Coordinator, Archdiocese of Boston); Natalie O'Connor (Director, Cambridge Spanish Council); Ann O'Donnell (Supervisory Head Teacher, Bilingual Program, Lowell Public Schools); Luis G. Perez (Probation Officer, Superior Court, Worcester Probation Department); Maria Reyes (Chief Elementary and Secondary Education Branch, Office for Civil Rights, Department of Health, Education and Welfare, Boston); Zaida Rivera (Executive Director, Lowell Area Ministries to People (LAMP)); Dr. Rene Romain (Disability Examiner, Social Security Disability Office, Boston); Dr. Robert Saitz (Professor of English, English Department, College of Liberal Arts, Boston University); Dr. David Shih (Chinese Education Committee, Brookline); Dr. Charles Smith (Director, Urban Education Studies, Boston College); Peter S. Stamas (Sub-master, Keith Extension, Lowell High School); Benedicto Toledo (Curriculum Coordinator, Lawrence Public Schools); Yolanda Ulloa (Bilingual Supervisor, Springfield Public Schools); Mary Vermette (Bilingual Director, Southeastern Massachusetts University, North Dartmouth); Dr. Silvia Viera (Director, Bilingual/Bicultural Education Professions Program, School of Education, University of Massachusetts, Amherst).

[13] Since nationally this is called "limited English proficient" (LEP), we use that term as well.

[14] In Massachusetts districts, LEP students are somewhat more concentrated in the elementary grades. Seventy-one percent of Spanish LEP students and 62 percent of the other LEP students are in grades K-6; this amounts to two students per grade at the elementary level and one per grade in high school. Data are from the 1993 Massachusetts Executive Office of Education Survey.

[15] See Christine Rossell and Keith Baker, "Selecting and exiting students in bilingual education programs," *Journal of Law and Education* (1988), 17 (4):589-23; J. Ramirez, S. Yuen, D. Ramey, and D. Pasta, *Final Report: Longitudinal Study of Structured English Immersion Strategy, Early-Exit and Late-Exit Transitional Bilingual Education Programs for Language-Minority Children*, Vol. I, prepared for U.S. Department of Education, San Mateo, CA: Aguirre International, 1991; J. Ramirez, D. Pasta, S. Yuen, D. Billings, and D. Ramey, *Final Report: Longitudinal Study of Structured English Immersion Strategy, Early-Exit and Late-Exit*

Transitional Bilingual Education Programs for Language-Minority Children, Vol. II, prepared for U.S. Department of Education, San Mateo, CA: Aguirre International, 1991; Christine Rossell, "Nothing Matters? A Critique of the Ramirez et al. Longitudinal Study of Instructional Programs for Language-Minority Children," *Bilingual Research Journal* (1992), 16 (1&2):159-186; Charles L. Glenn, "How We are Failing 'Linguistic Minority' Students," *Equity and* Choice (Spring 1986), 2(3):79-86.

[16] See page 13 of Educating Language Minority Students: Laws, Regulations, Policies and Guidelines in the Commonwealth of Massachusetts, Quincy, MA: Massachusetts Department of Education, December 1992.

[17] The requirement for a TBE director or supervisor if a TBE program enrolls more than 200 students is, we believe, a subtle acknowledgment on the part of the state DOE that any fewer than that for a single language group is not a real bilingual program (although that number still does not guarantee native tongue instruction in a self-contained classroom).

[18] *Educating Language Minority Students*, Massachusetts Department of Education, December 1992:43.

[19] Again, the notion that districts with more than 200 students in a TBE program need more monitoring is an implicit recognition that these districts are more likely to have real TBE programs.

[20] See, for example, David J. Armor, *Forced Justice: School Desegregation and the Law*, New York: Oxford University Press, 1995: 59-116.

[21] Bilingual Education Commission, *Striving for Success: The Education of Bilingual Pupils*, Boston, MA: Commonwealth of Massachusetts, December 1994.

[22] The 1992 NAEP mathematics assessment included nearly 250,000 randomly selected fourth, eighth, and twelfth grade students. The National Assessment Governing Board established three achievement levels for reporting NAEP results: Basic, Proficient, and Advanced. The Basic Level denotes partial mastery of the knowledge and skills fundamental for Proficient grade at each level. Proficient, the central level, represents the solid fundamental performance and demonstrated competence over challenging subject matter. This is the achievement level the Board has determined all students should reach. National Center for Education Statistics, *NAEP 1992 Mathematics Report Card for the Nation and the States*, Washington, D.C.: Government Printing Office, 1992.

[23] It should be noted that there is an error in the figures reported in Commonwealth of Massachusetts, *The Condition of Education 1994*, Chart 4E on page 4-14. The figures reported in our book come from the original document, National Center for Education Statistics, 1992, and are correct.

[24] Commonwealth of Massachusetts, *The Condition of Education 1994*, charts 13-15, pp. 0-9; Massachusetts Department of Education, Office of

Planning, Research and Evaluation, Individual School Report, October 1, 1994, table 3.

CHAPTER THREE: THE EDUCATIONAL EFFECTIVENESS OF BILINGUAL EDUCATION

[1] Kenji Hakuta, *Mirror of Language, The Debate on Bilingualism,* New York: Basic Books, 1986: 219.

[2] T.P. Carter and M.L. Chatfield, "Effective Bilingual Schools: Implications for Policy and Practice," *American Journal of Education* (1986), 95: 210.

[3] C.B. Paulston (ed.), *Swedish Research and Debate About Bilingualism: A Critical Review of the Swedish Research and Debate about Bilingualism and Bilingual Education in Sweden From an International Perspective,* Report to the National Swedish Board of Education, 1982: 47-48.

[4] P. Toukomaa, "Education through the Medium of the Mother Tongue of Finnish Immigrant Children," in C. B. Paulston (ed.), *Swedish Research and Debate about Bilingualism,* 1982: 103.

[5] *Building an Indivisible Nation: Bilingual Education in Context,* Alexandria, VA: Association for Supervision and Curriculum Development, 1987: 35.

[6] See R. Troike, "Research evidence for the effectiveness of bilingual education," *NABE Journal* (1978), 3 (1):13-4; P. Engle, "The use of the vernacular language in education," Bilingual education series No. 2, Washington, DC: Center for Applied Linguistics, 1975; Iris Rotberg, "Federal policy in bilingual education," *American Education* (1982), 52 (2):30-40; Ann C. Willig, "A Meta-Analysis of Selected Studies on the Effectiveness of Bilingual Education," *Review of Educational Research* (1985), 55 (3):269-317; J. Yates and A. Ortiz, "Baker & de Kanter review: Inappropriate conclusions on the efficacy of bilingual education," *Journal of the National Association for Bilingual Education* (1983), 7 (3):75-84; M. Peterson et al., "Assessment of the Status of Bilingual Vocational Training: Review of the Literature," *ERIC* (1976), 131:683; General Accounting Office (GAO), *Bilingual Education: A New Look at the Research Evidence,* Briefing Report to the Chairman, Committee on Education and Labor, House of Representatives, 1987; R. Holland, *Bilingual education: Recent evaluations of local school district programs and related research on second-language learning,* Washington, DC: Congressional Research Service, 1986; D. Ravitch, *The Troubled Crusade,* New York: Basic Books, 1983; H. Dulay and M. Burt, "From research to method in bilingual education," *Georgetown University Roundtable on Language and Linguistics,* Washington, DC: Georgetown University, 1978; L.T. Zappert and B.R.

Cruz, *Bilingual Education: An Appraisal of Empirical Research,* Berkeley, Calif.: The Berkeley Unified School District, 1977; P. Zirkel, *An evaluation of the effectiveness of selected experimental bilingual education programs in Connecticut,* Hartford, CT: Connecticut Department of Education, 1972.

[7] This chapter is a condensed version of Christine H. Rossell and Keith Baker, "The Educational Effectiveness of Bilingual Education," *Research in the Teaching of English* (February 1996), 30 (1):7-74. The original contains more detailed discussions of our methodology and the results of specific studies mentioned here. It also contains complete lists of the studies we reviewed categorized as methodologically acceptable or unacceptable.

[8] Christine Rossell and J. Michael Ross, "The social science evidence on bilingual education," *Journal of Law and Education* (1986), 15: 385-419; Keith Baker and Adriana de Kanter, *The effectiveness of bilingual education programs: A review of the literature, final draft report,* Washington, DC: U.S. Department of Education, 1981; Keith Baker and Adriana de Kanter, "An answer from research on bilingual education," *American Education* (1983), 56 (4):157-169; Keith Baker and Adriana de Kanter, "Federal Policy and the Effectiveness of Bilingual Education," in Keith A. Baker, Adriana A. de Kanter (eds.), *Bilingual Education,* Lexington, MA: D.C. Heath and Company, 1983.

[9] The initial list of studies on bilingual education was obtained from a search of the Educational Research Information Clearinghouse (ERIC) documents, the Boston University, MIT, Boston College, and the Boston Public Library card catalogues, Language and Language Behavior Abstracts, and the bibliographies of other reviews of the literature. The studies actually reviewed were those that could be obtained from 1) ERIC; 2) University Microfilms International; 3) the journal and book holdings of Boston University, MIT, Boston College, and the Boston Public Library; 4) the National Clearinghouse on Bilingual Education; 5) the Center for Applied Linguistics; 6) the Department of Education; 7) the authors themselves; 8) interlibrary loan; and 9) program evaluations for 1991-93 obtained by writing to school districts in the United States. Not all studies are documented, nor could all documented studies be obtained.

[10] See Rossell and Baker (1996) for a list of studies that discuss each of these factors.

[11] Analysis of covariance is a statistical technique that determines whether the difference in the mean outcome (e.g., achievement) for two or more groups (e.g., students in a bilingual education program compared to those in another program) is significantly different after adjusting for another variable (the covariate) thought to be correlated with the outcome, for example, the achievement of each student before entering the program.

[12] Marcello Medina and Kathy Escamilla, "Evaluation of Transitional and Maintenance Bilingual Programs," *Urban Education* (1992), 27 (3):263-290. Ramirez et al. (1991) also examined maintenance bilingual education (late-exit bilingual education) but unfortunately did not directly compare it to transitional bilingual education (contrary to media reports and his own conclusions). Although his graphs appeared to show that the students in late-exit bilingual education were doing worse than the students in transitional bilingual education, no statistical analysis was performed to verify that. J. Ramirez, S. Yuen, D. Ramey, and D. Pasta, *Final Report: Longitudinal Study of Structured English Immersion Strategy, Early-Exit and Late-Exit Transitional Bilingual Education Programs for Language-Minority Children*, Vol. I, prepared for U.S. Department of Education, San Mateo, CA: Aguirre International, 1991; J. Ramirez, D. Pasta, S. Yuen, D. Billings, and D. Ramey, *Final Report: Longitudinal Study of Structured English Immersion Strategy, Early-Exit and Late-Exit Transitional Bilingual Education Programs for Language-Minority Children*, Vol. II, prepared for U.S. Department of Education, San Mateo, CA: Aguirre International, 1991.

[13] G. Richard Tucker, Wallace E. Lambert, and A. d'Anglejan, "French Immersion Programs: A Pilot Investigation," *Language Sciences* (1973), 25:19-26; Margaret Bruck, Jola Jakimik, and G. Richard Tucker, "Are French Immersion Programs Suitable for Working-Class Children? A Follow-up Investigation," *Word* (1971), 27:311-341; Gary A. Cziko, "The Effects of Different French Immersion Programs on the Language and Academic Skills of Children from Various Socioeconomic Backgrounds," M.A. thesis, McGill University, 1975; Fred Genesee, "The Suitability of Immersion Programs for all Children," *Canadian Modern Language Review* (1976), 32:494-515.

[14] Leonard A. Popp, "The English Competence of French Speaking Students in a Bilingual Setting," *Canadian Modern Language Review* (1976), 32:365-377; G. Richard Tucker, "Implications for U.S. Bilingual Education: Evidence from Canadian Research," National Clearinghouse for Bilingual Education, *NCBE Focus* (1980), 2:1-3; M. Swain, "Time and timing in bilingual education," *Language Learning* (1981), 31:1; Eduardo Hernandez-Chavez, "The Inadequacy of English Immersion Education as an Educational Approach for Language Minority Students in the United States," in *Studies on Immersion Education,* Sacramento: California State Department of Education, 1984.

[15] Baker and de Kanter (1981, 1983a, 1983b), Engle (1975), Rotberg (1982), Holland (1986), Rossell and Ross (1986), and N. Epstein, *Language, Ethnicity and the Schools: Policy Alternatives for Bilingual-Bicultural Education,* Washington, D.C.: Institute for Educational

Leadership, 1977, have also concluded there is no research support for transitional bilingual education.

[16] Zappert and Cruz, 1977: 8.

[17] J. Cummins, "Educational implications of mother tongue maintenance in minority language groups," *Canadian Modern Language Review* (1978), 34:395-416; J. Cummins, "The role of primary language development in promoting educational success for language minority students," in California State Department of Education (Comp.), *Schooling and language minority students: A theoretical framework,* Los Angeles: UCLA Evaluation, Dissemination, and Assessment Center, 1981; J. Cummins, "The construct of language proficiency in bilingual education," in *Perspectives on Bilingualism and Bilingual Education,* Washington, DC: Georgetown University Press, 1985.

[18] Perhaps one of the more serious flaws of the facilitation theory is its lack of attention to non-Roman or non-alphabetic languages that have no similarity to English in appearance and take much longer to master. Learning to read in the native language may actually be harder in these languages than in the second language, if the latter is English or another roman alphabet language. We know of no non-roman alphabet bilingual programs in the United States that actually teach initial literacy in the native language, although many of them are nevertheless called bilingual education and receive bilingual education funding. Russian, for one, is apparently more difficult to master than English. Slobin (1966) found that the Russian-speaking child does not fully master his morphology until he is several years older than the age at which an English-speaking child does. Dan I. Slobin, "The Acquisition of Russian as a Native Language," in Frank Smith and George A. Miller (eds.), *The Genesis of Language,* Cambridge, MA: MIT Press, 1966: 129-52, cited in Izzo, 1981.

[19] Cummins cites a UNESCO study, *The Use of the Vernacular Languages in Education* (Monographs on Fundamental Education, 1953), but there is no reference to this study in any of the legislation or literature of the 1960s.

[20] S. Izzo, *Second Language Learning: A Review of Related Studies,* Virginia: National Clearinghouse for Bilingual Education, 1981:51-52.

[21] J.B. Carroll, "Commentary," in "The Ottawa-Carleton French project: Issues, conclusions, and policy implications," in H.H. Stern (ed.), *Canadian Modern Language Review* (1976), 32:235.

[22] J. Cummins and R. Mulcahy, *Orientation to language in Ukrainian-English bilinguals,* University of Alberta, 1977. Aside from the issue of the importance of the task, this study can tell us nothing about the kind of instruction LEP children should receive since the fluent Ukrainian bilingual students not only did better than the monolingual controls, but they also did better than the non-fluent Ukrainian bilingual students who were receiving *identical* instruction. It is likely that other factors—such as intelligence levels—would explain these results.

[23] D. Leslie, "Bilingual Education and Native Canadians," research report, University of Alberta, 1977. This only further underscores the extent to which these studies simply test native intelligence since there is no pedagogical theory that argues high native tongue *oral* fluency stimulates higher second language *reading* levels.

[24] E. Hebert and Others, "Academic achievement, language of instruction, and the Franco-Manitoban student," College Universitaire de St. Boniface: Centre de Recherches, 1976; A.G Ramirez and R.L. Politzer, "The acquisition of English and the maintenance of Spanish in a bilingual education program," in J. Atlatis and Twaddell (eds.), *English as a Second Language in Bilingual Education,* Washington, D.C.: Teachers of English to Speakers of Other Languages, 1976. Although Cummins' theories are widely cited in the United States as evidence for the superiority of TBE, he relies on research on *bilingualism* conducted in Canada, where the educational process of creating bilinguals is the reverse of the United States. There, in the most common and successful program, students are taught completely in the second language in kindergarten and first grade and gradually transitioned to mostly the native tongue by high school. Although everyone believes these programs to be quite successful, Cummins continues to be cited as evidence for the superiority of the U.S. version of bilingual education—the native tongue first and a gradual transition to the second language.

[25] Tove Skutnabb-Kangas and P. Toukomaa, "Teaching migrant children's mother tongue and learning the language of the host country in the context of the socio-cultural situation of the migrant family," New York: UNESCO, 1976.

[26] See Baker and de Kanter, 1981.

[27] Collier has conducted one of the few studies that directly attempts to test Cummins' hypotheses and, as with many studies of bilingual education, her data contradict the theory she purports to have proved. Because it is widely cited as support for the facilitation theory, however, it is worth discussing here although we have classified it as methodologically unacceptable in Rossell and Baker (1996). Collier tested Cummins' hypothesis that there is a facilitation effect of the native tongue on the second language with 20 pseudo-learning curves derived from cross-sectional achievement data of students who had been in the United States for varying amounts of time. (She incorrectly describes these as "rates" of learning. Since they are cross-sectional rather than longitudinal data, she cannot show rates of learning but only levels of achievement at a particular point in time.) If the facilitation hypothesis is correct, these curves should be negatively accelerated—that is the shorter the length of residence in the United States for students 8 years or older, the higher the achievement in English. Of the 20 curves, however, only two (or perhaps three) clearly show negative ac-

celeration. About eight curves show *positive* acceleration. If one simplifies the problem of interpreting the curves by asking only if the two end points of the curve show negative acceleration, there are eight that support the hypothesis and 12 that contradict it.

There is a second way in which Collier's results contradict Cummins. Collier claimed evidence of the facilitation effect for children aged 8 to 11 because she could not find it in children aged 12 to 16, which is where Cummins says it occurs. Thus, one of the few researchers to directly test Cummins' theory finds contrary evidence, but, because of the importance of the facilitation effect for transitional bilingual education, urges us to discount her findings instead. V. Collier, *The effect of age on acquisition of a second language for school,* Washington, DC: National Clearinghouse for Bilingual Education, 1987; V. Collier, "Age and rate of acquisition of second language for academic purposes," *TESOL Quarterly* (1987), 214:617-641.

Several other researchers have directly or indirectly tested the facilitation effect. The Eastman Project is perhaps the major effort to demonstrate the facilitation hypothesis. Although Krashen and Biber claim to support the facilitation hypothesis, their analysis is so severely flawed that no conclusions can be drawn from it. S. Krashen and D. Biber, "On Course: Bilingual Education's Success in California," Sacramento: California Association for Bilingual Education, 1988. For a critique of Krashen and Biber, see Keith Baker, "Bilingual education's 20-year failure to provide civil rights protection for language minority students," in A. Barona and E. Garcia (eds.), *Children at risk: Poverty, minority status, and other issues in educational equity,* Washington, DC: National Association of School Psychologists, 1990.

[28] W.E. Lambert and G.R. Tucker, *Bilingual education of children: The St. Lambert experience,* Rowley, MA: Newbury House, 1972; H. Barik and M. Swain, "Three year evaluation of a large scale early grade French immersion program: the Ottawa study," *Language Learning* (1975), 25 (1); M. Bruck, W. Lambert, and R. Tucker, "Cognitive consequences of bilingual schooling: The St. Lambert project through grade six," *Linguistics* (1977):13-32.

[29] D. Ausubel, "Adults versus children in second language learning," *Modern Language Journal* (1964), 48:420; B. Taylor, "Toward a theory of language acquisition," *Language Learning* (1974), 24:23; S. Ervin-Tripp, "Is second language learning like the first?" *Tesol Quarterly* (1974), 8:11; H. Stern, C. Burstall, and B. Harley, *French from age eight, or eleven?* Toronto, Ont.: Ontario Ministry of Education, 1975; L.H. Eckstrand, "Age and length of residence as variables related to the adjustments of migrant children with special reference to second language learning," paper presented at the Association Internationale de Linguistique Appliquee Con-

gress, Stuttgart, 1975; A.G. Ramirez and R.L. Politzer, "Comprehension and Production in English as a Second Language by Elementary School Children and Adolescents," in E.M. Hatch (ed.), *Second language acquisition: A book of readings,* 1978; Swain, 1981.

[30] See, for example, P. Rosier and M. Farella, "Bilingual education at rock point: Some early results," *TESOL Quarterly* (1976), 10:379; P. Rosier and W. Holm, *The Rock Point experience: A longitudinal study of a Navajo school program* (saad naaki bee na'nitin), Arlington, VA: Center for Applied Linguistics, 1980; Skutnabb-Kangas and Toukomaa, 1976.

[31] See Izzo, 1981.

[32] Ramirez et al., 1991. Keith Baker was the project officer at the US Department of Education for the Ramirez et al. (1991) study.

[33] One of the two main mistakes of the Ramirez et al. (1991) study was the use of nominal program designation—early-exit TBE, late-exit TBE, and structured immersion—as the treatment variable rather than the percentage of English used in instruction, which varied considerably within nominal program categories and by subject matter. The second mistake was the failure to directly compare with statistical analyses the late-exit program to the early-exit and immersion programs. See Christine Rossell, "Nothing Matters? A Critique of the Ramírez, et al. Longitudinal Study of Instructional Programs for Language-Minority Children," *Bilingual Research Journal* (1992), 16 (1&2):159-186; Keith Baker, "Ramírez et al.: Led by Bad Theory," *Bilingual Research Journal* (1992), 16 (1&2):91-104; M. Meyer and S. Fienberg (eds.), *Assessing Evaluation Studies: The case of bilingual education strategies,* Washington, D.C.: National Academy Press, 1992.

[34] G.J. Burkheimer, Jr., A. Conger, G. Dunteman, B. Elliott, and K. Mowbray, "Effectiveness of services for language minority limited English proficient students," Raleigh-Durham, NC.: Research Triangle Institute, 1989: 5.43.

[35] L.W. Fillmore, "Learning a Second Language: Chinese children in the American Classroom," *Georgetown University Roundtable on Language and Linguistics,* Washington, D.C.: Georgetown University Press, 1980.

[36] K. Carsrud and J. Curtis, *ESEA Title VII Bilingual Program: Final Report,* Austin, Texas: Austin Independent School District, 1980.

[37] W.J. Tickunoff, *An emerging description of successful bilingual instruction: executive summary of part I of the SBIF study,* San Francisco: Far West Laboratory for Educational Research and Development, 1983.

[38] G. Ligon et al., *ESAA bilingual/bicultural project,* 1973-74 evaluation report, Austin: Austin Independent School District, 1974; J. Curtis, "Identification of exemplary teachers of LEP students," paper presented at the annual meeting of the American Educational Research Association, New Orleans, April 1984.

[39] Malcolm N. Danoff, Beatiz M. Arias, Gary J. Coles et al., *Evaluation of the impact of ESEA Title VII Spanish/English Bilingual education program,* Palo Alto: American Institutes for Research, 1977; Malcolm N. Danoff, Gary J. Coles, Donald H. McLaughlin, and Dorothy J. Reynolds, *Evaluation of the impact of ESEA Title VII Spanish/English bilingual education program,* Palo Alto: American Institutes for Research, 1978.

[40] Christine Rossell, "The Effectiveness of Educational Alternatives for Limited-English-Proficient Children," in *Learning in Two Languages,* New Brunswick: Transaction Publishers, 1990.

[41] F.B. Moore and G.D. Parr, "Models of bilingual education: Comparisons of effectiveness," *The Elementary School Journal* (1978), 79:93-97.

[42] For the most recent example of this, see Rosalie Porter, *Forked Tongue,* New York: Basic Books, 1990; Rosalie Porter, "Reflections on the politics of bilingual education," *Journal of Law and Politics* (1990), 6 (3):573-599.

[43] For example, D. Wiley, "Another hour, another day: Quantity of schooling, a potent path for society," in W. Sewell, R. Hauser, and D. Featherman (eds.), *Schooling and achievement in American society,* New York: Academic Press, 1976; B.V. Rosenshine, "Content, time and direct instruction," in P. Peterson and H. Walberg (eds.), in *Research on Teaching: Concepts, Findings and Implications*, Berkeley: McCutcheon, 1979; K. Clauset and A. Gaynor, *Closing the Learning Gap: Effective Schooling for Initially Low Achievers,* Boston University, 1980.

[44] C.W. Fisher et al., "Teaching behaviors, academic learning time and student achievement: an overview," in C. Denham and A. Leiberman (eds.), *Time to Learn,* Washington, D.C.: Department of Health, Education, and Welfare, National Institute of Education, 1980; N. Karweit, *Time on task: A research review,* Washington, DC: National Commission on Educational Excellence, 1983.

[45] See also S. Krashen, "The input hypothesis," in J. Alatis (ed.), *Georgetown University Round Table on Language and Linguistics,* Washington, D.C.: Georgetown University, 1980; M. Long, "Input, Interaction and Second Language Acquisition," *Annals of the New York Academy of Science,* New York: New York Academy of Science, 1981; M. Swain, "Communicative competence. Some roles of comprehensible input and comprehensible output in its development," paper presented at the Second Language Research Forum, University of California, Los Angeles, November 1983.

[46] Rossell, 1990.

[47] C. Duncan, "The effect of unequal amounts of practice on motor learning before and after rest," *Journal of Experimental Psychology* (1951), 42:257-264.

[48] Because of the influence of the facilitation theory, however, it is not always the case that English will be part of the instructional program. Christine Rossell has personally observed dozens of kindergarten, and to a lesser extent first grade, classrooms in Massachusetts where almost no English at all is used in instruction. The teachers justify this on the grounds that their students need a long time to develop a high level of native tongue proficiency—a prerequisite to future academic success in the all-English classroom. In short, they are true believers of the facilitation theory even if they may not know its name.

CHAPTER FOUR: EVERY CLASSROOM IS AN ISLAND

[1] See p. 129 of U.S. Bureau of the Census, "The Foreign-Born Population in the U.S.," Washington, DC: Government Printing Office, July 1993.

[2] See tables 4 and 5 of Massachusetts Department of Education, Office of Planning, Research And Evaluation, Individual School Report, October 1, 1992.

[3] U.S. Bureau of the Census, "The Foreign-Born Population in the U.S.," July 1993:129; U.S. Bureau of the Census, 1990 Census; Statistical Abstract of the U.S., 1991, table 222; Massachusetts Department of Education, Individual School Report, October 1, 1992, tables 3, 4, 5.

[4] Data on the language minority (first language not English) and LEP population in the 286 school districts in Massachusetts that had at least one language minority student are reported for seven language groups (Spanish, Khmer, Portuguese, Chinese, Vietnamese, Cape Verdean, and Haitian) plus "other" in the annual October "Individual School Reports," tables 4 and 5. In the 51 districts with 20 or more of a single language group, data on the incidence of LEP classification and enrollment in TBE are available for 80 language groups and by district. These data come from the Transitional Bilingual Education Report published in June of each school year. As of the writing of this book, the latest year for which these data were available is 1992-93.

[5] U.S. Bureau of the Census, "The Foreign-Born Population in the United States," (1990 CP-3-1), 1993.

[6] Unfortunately, it is not possible to calculate the LEP rate for Asian, black, and white students because LEP statistics are not kept finely enough for these groups. Asians, for example, are represented by only three language groups—Khmer, Cantonese, and Vietnamese—in the Massachusetts statistics. Blacks are represented in the Massachusetts statistics by only two language groups—Cape Verdean and Haitian. Then there is a residual category called "other." There is even less information at the national level. Massachusetts Department of Education, Individual School Report, October 1, 1992, tables 3, 4, 5; Statistical Abstract of the United States,

1991, table 222; Howard L. Fleischman and Paul J. Hopstick, "*Descriptive Study of Services to Limited English Proficient Students: Volume I, Summary of Findings and Conclusions*," Arlington, VA: Development Associates, Inc., prepared for U.S. Department of Education, 1993:11.

[7] However, there is no such thing as a spoken language called "Chinese." If these programs were to be conducted in the native tongue, they would have to be in Cantonese, Mandarin, or Toisan (or any of the hundreds of other dialects spoken throughout China), and there are rarely enough native speakers of any of these dialects to fill a classroom. Thus, one can generally assume that any TBE program called "Chinese" is not conducted in the native tongue.

[8] The classroom observations and interviews in Massachusetts were conducted between 1992 and 1994 by Christine Rossell, who has been observing bilingual education classrooms for many years, both in Massachusetts and in California. The observations lasted on average one-half hour and covered more than 75 separate classrooms. We have not listed the districts whose programs were observed, as several requested anonymity.

[9] The statistics on numbers of LEP students of each language minority group cited in the classroom observations section come from table 2, "Detail of Districts Within Languages," of Massachusetts Department of Education, *Transitional Bilingual Education Report, year ending June 30, 1993*.

[10] J. Ramirez, S. Yuen, D. Ramey, and D. Pasta, *Final Report: Longitudinal Study of Structured English Immersion Strategy, Early-Exit and Late-Exit Transitional Bilingual Education Programs for Language-Minority Children*, Vol. I, prepared for U.S. Department of Education, San Mateo, CA: Aguirre International, 1991; J. Ramirez, D. Pasta, S. Yuen, D. Billings, and D. Ramey, *Final Report: Longitudinal Study of Structured English Immersion Strategy, Early-Exit and Late-Exit Transitional Bilingual Education Programs for Language-Minority Children*, Vol. II, prepared for U.S. Department of Education, San Mateo, CA: Aguirre International, 1991.

[11] "Preliminary Survey: Transitional Bilingual Education," Executive Office of Education, Commonwealth of Massachusetts, January 1993.

Chapter Five: Selecting and Exiting Students in Bilingual Education Programs

[1] J.B. Carroll, "Fundamental Considerations in Testing for English Language Proficiency of Foreign Students," in Harold B. Allen (ed.), *Teaching English as a Second Language: A Book of Readings,* New York: McGraw-Hill, 1972.

[2] Eugene Briere, "Are We Really Measuring Proficiency with Our Foreign Language Tests?" *Foreign Language Annuals* (1971), 4: 385-391; Donn R. Callaway, "Accent and the Evaluation of ESL Oral Proficiency," in John W. Oller and Kyle Perkins (ed.), *Research in Language Testing,* Rowley, MA: Newbury House, 1980; Kay K. Hisma, "An Analysis of Various ESL Proficiency Tests," in John W. Oller and Kyle Perkins (ed.), *Research in Language Testing,* Rowley, MA: Newbury House, 1980.

[3] Ernest Bernal, "Issues Related to the Assessment of Chicano Children," Proceedings of With Bias Towards None: A National Planning Conference on Nondiscriminatory Assessment for Handicapped Children, 1975; Ernest Bernal, "Assessment Procedures for Chicano Children: The Sad State of the Art," *Aztlan* (1979), 8: 69-81.

[4] A. Hilliard, "Standardized Testing and Non-standard Population," *The Generator of AERA* (1981).

[5] A. Law, "Evaluating Bilingual Programs," Tests and Measurements Report 61, ERIC Clearinghouse on Tests, Measurements, and Evaluation, 1977; Southwest Educational Regional Laboratories (SWERL), "Designers Manual: Resources for Developing a Student Placement System for Bilingual Programs," Austin, Texas, 1980.

[6] See, for example, F. Howard Nelson, "The Assessment of English Language Proficiency: Standards for Determining Participation in Transitional Language Programs," *Journal of Law and Education* (1986), 15: 83-103.

[7] See Keith Baker and Christine Rossell, "An Implementation Problem: Specifying the Target Group for Bilingual Education," *Educational Policy* (1987), 1 (2): 249-270; Christine Rossell and Keith Baker, "Selecting and Exiting Students in Bilingual Educational Programs," *Journal of Law and Education* (1988), 17 (4): 589-623.

[8] Bilingual Education Act, Pub. L. 95-561, 20 USC 3223 (92 STAT. 2270).

[9] Title VII is now called Bilingual Education, Language Enhancement, and Language Acquisition Programs.

[10] Bilingual Education, Language Enhancement, and Language Acquisition Programs, Pub. L. 103-382, Section 7102, 14 (c).

[11] Pub. L. 103-382, section 7501 (8).

[12] Chapter 71A, Transitional Bilingual Education, section 2, reprinted in, *Educating Language Minority Students; Laws, Regulations, Policies and Guidelines in the Commonwealth of Massachusetts,* Quincy, MA: Massachusetts Department of Education, December 1992: 7.

[13] Their study included the District of Columbia, Northern Mariana Islands, and the Virgin Islands, in addition to the 50 states. Onna M. Cheung and Lisa W. Solomon, "Summary of State Practices Concerning the Assessment of and the Data Collection about Limited English Proficient

(LEP) Students," Washington, D.C.: Council of Chief State School Officers, 1991.

[14] Letter, Elizabeth Twomey, Associate Commissioner, School Programs, and Gilman Hebert, Director, Bureau of Equity and Language Services, to Superintendents, Transitional Bilingual Education Directors, December 26, 1990, Quincy, Massachusetts.

[15] Cheung and Solomon, 1991:36.

[16] *Educating Language Minority Students,* Commonwealth of Massachusetts, December 1992:7.

[17] Cheung and Solomon, 1991:39.

[18] Betty J. Mace-Matluck, "Teaching Reading in the Bilingual Program with Emphasis on Transferability of Spanish Reading Skills to English Reading," paper presented at San Diego State University BESC Multidistrict Preservice Workshop, San Diego, California, 1982.

[19] D. Cardoza, "The Reclassification Survey: A Study of Entry and Exit Classification Procedures," Los Alamitos, CA: National Center for Bilingual Research, 1984.

[20] Malcolm B. Young, Paul Hopstock, Milton R. Goldsamt, et al., "Final Report, Descriptive Study Phase, The National Longitudinal Evaluation of the Effectiveness of Services for Language-Minority Limited-English-Proficient Students," Arlington, VA: Development Associates and Research Triangle Park, NC: Research Triangle Institute, 1984.

[21] These include the Amherst Kindergarten Screening, the Eliot Pearson Screening, the Step Up to Reading Diagnostic Assessment, the Murphy Durrell, the Gates Macginities, the Amherst Cloze Test, the Woodcock, the Informal Reading Inventory (Scott Foresman), the Durrell Analysis of Reading Difficulty, and the LAS.

[22] Bilingual Education Commission, *Striving for Success: The Education of Bilingual Pupils,* Boston, MA: Commonwealth of Massachusetts, December 1994.

[23] See Rossell and Baker (1988) for discussion of these cases.

[24]See, for example, James Coleman et al., *Equality of Educational Opportunity,* Washington DC: Government Printing Office, 1966; David J. Armor, *Forced Justice: School Desegregation and the Law,* New York: Oxford University Press, 1995; Christopher Jencks, *Inequality,* New York: Basic Books, 1972; Frederick Mosteller and Daniel P. Moynihan, *On Equality of Educational Opportunity,* New York: Vintage Books, 1972; Gerald Jaynes and Robin Williams, Jr., *Common Destiny: Blacks and American Society,* Washington, DC: National Academy Press, 1989; David Grissmer et al., *Student Achievement and the Changing American Family,* The Rand Corporation, 1994.

[25] Another problem with using standardized tests to identify students needing bilingual education is that the entry decision test score for students

who truly are limited in English proficiency will be extremely unreliable since it has an enormous error-score component and almost no true score component. In other words, if a student knows little or no English, the test score will be based almost entirely on guessing.

[26] Texas Education Agency, "Report of the Committee for the Evaluation of Language Assessment Instruments," Austin, TX, 1977; Texas Education Agency, "Report of the Committee for the Evaluation of Language Assessment Instruments," Austin, TX, 1979; J.David Ramirez, Barbara Merino, Thomas Bye, and Norman Gold, "Assessment of Oral Language Proficiency", unpublished manuscript, SRA Technologies, Mountain View, CA, 1981.

[27] Northwest Regional Educational Laboratory (NWREL), "Assessment Instruments in Bilingual Education: A Descriptive Catalogue of 342 Oral and Written Tests," Portland, OR, 1978; NWREL, "Oral Language Tests for Bilingual Students: An Evaluation of Oral Language Dominance and Proficiency Instruments," Portland, OR, 1976; Dissemination and Assessment Center for Bilingual Education (DACBE), *Evaluation Instruments for Bilingual Education: An Annotated Bibliography,* Austin, TX, 1976; Thomas T. Bye, "Tests that Measure Language Ability: A Descriptive Compilation," Berkeley, CA: Babel/Lau Center, 1977; A. Law, "Proceedings of the Bilingual Instrument Review Committee (AB 3470)," Sacramento, CA: California State Department of Education, Office of Program Evaluation and Research, 1978; Barbara Pletcher, Nancy A. Locks, Dorothy F. Reynolds, and Bonnie G. Sisson, *A Guide to Assessment Instruments for Limited English Speaking Students,* New York: Santillana Publishing Co., 1978; J. Curtis, G. Lignon, and G. Weibly, "When Is a LEP No Longer LEP?" paper delivered at the annual meeting of the American Educational Research Association, San Francisco, CA, 1979; D.P Horst, D.E. Douglas, L.D. Friendly, D.M. Johnson, L.M. Luber, J. McKay, H.G. Nava, A.M. Piestrup, A.O.H. Roberts, and A. Valdez, "An Evaluation of Product Information Packages (PIPS) as Used for the Diffusion of Bilingual Research Projects, Vols. I and II," Mountain View, CA: RMC Research Corporation, 1980 (UR-460); D.P Horst, D.M. Johnson, H.G. Nava, D.E. Douglas, L.D. Friendly, I.M. Luber, J. Mckay, and A.O.H. Roberts, "A Prototype Guide to Measuring Achievement Level And Program Impact on Achievement in Bilingual Projects," in D.P. Horst et al. (eds.), "An Evaluation of Product Information Packages (PIPS) as Used for the Diffusion of Bilingual Research Projects (Vol. III)," Mountain View, CA: RMC Research Corporation, 1980; Massachusetts Bureau of Transitional Bilingual Education, "General Framework and Criteria for the Development of Statewide English and Language Proficiency Test for Limited English Proficiency Students, K-12," Boston, MA: State Advisory Council on Bilingual Education, 1987.

[28] Twomey and Hebert to Superintendents, December 26, 1990.

[29] Jim Cummins, "Policy Report: Language and Literacy in Bilingual Instruction," Austin, TX: Southwest Educational Development Laboratory, 1983, NIE Contract No. 400-80-0043; M. Canale, "On Some Dimensions of Language Proficiency," in John W. Oller (ed.), *Issues in Language Testing Research*, Rowley, MA: Newbury House, 1983; D. Ulibarri, M. Spencer, and G. Rivas, "Language Proficiency and Academic Achievement: A Study of Language Proficiency Tests and Their Relationship to School Ratings as Predictors of Achievement," *NABE Journal* (1981) 5: 47-80; D. Ulibarri, M. Spencer, and G. Rivas, "Comparability of Three Oral Language Proficiency Instruments and Their Relationship to Achievement Variables," report submitted to the California State Department of Education, 1980.

[30] Barnard Spolsky, *Educational Linguistics,* Rowley, MA: Newbury House Publishers, 1978: 115 cited in National Institute of Education (NIE), "Report on the Testing and Assessment Implications of the Title VI Language Minority Proposed Rules," Washington, D.C., 1981: 38.

[31] NIE, 1981: 38.

[32] S. Irujo, C. Kramsch, N.C. Dube, and J. Yedlin, "Language Proficiency," presented at Language and the World of Work in the Twenty-First Century symposium sponsored by the Bureau of Transitional Bilingual Education, Massachusetts Department of Education, Boston, 1986.

[33] G. Gillmore and A. Dickerson, "The Relationship Between Instruments Used for Identifying Children of Limited English Speaking Ability in Texas," Houston, Texas: Education Service Center [Region IV], 1979; Robert A. Cervantes, "Bilingual Program Exit Criteria, in 2 Bilingual Resources," Los Angeles, CA: University of California, National Dissemination and Assessment Center, 1979; Robert A. Cervantes, *Entry into and Exit from Bilingual Education Programs,* Washington, D.C.: E.H. White Inc., 1982.

[34] Sol Pelavin and Keith Baker, "Improved Methods of Identifying Who Needs Bilingual Education," paper prepared for delivery at the annual meeting of the American Educational Research Association, Washington, D.C., 1987; Sol Pelavin, Keith Baker, Carin A. Celebuski, Linda Fink, "Determining Which Non-English Language Background Students Need Special Language Services," paper prepared for delivery at the annual meeting of the American Educational Research Association, Washington, D.C., 1988.

[35] The school district administered it to both Title I and bilingual education students. The Title I students passed it, while the bilingual education students failed it.

[36] Barry McLaughlin and Lily Wong-Fillmore, "A Functional Approach to Language Assessment: the Shell and Rock Games," paper presented at

the annual meeting of the National Association for Bilingual Education, San Francisco, California, 1985.

[37] For the purposes of their analysis, Pelavin and Associates used the following classification: 1) LAS: below 5 is LEP; 2) MEC: below 6 is LEP; 3) Shell: students were rated as either LEP or English proficient; and 4) LAB: LEP is below 25 for kindergarten, 44 for first grade, 53 for second grade, 69 for third grade, 72 for fourth grade, 76 for fifth grade, and 80 for sixth grade.

[38] J. David Ramirez, Sandra D. Yuen, and Dena Ramey, "Second Year Report: Study of Immersion Programs for Language Minority Children," Alexandria, VA: SRA Technologies, Inc., 1986.

[39] Alvin S. Rosenthal, Keith Baker, and Alan Ginsburg, "The Effect of Language Background on Achievement Level and Learning Among Elementary School Students," *Sociology of Education* (1983), 56: 157-169.

[40] These results apply to Hispanics as a group, not to individual Hispanic students who may not speak English. Mayeske's results are undoubtedly a function of the fact that there are so few Hispanic background students who do not speak English that their effect on the class as a whole cannot be detected. G.W. Mayeske, M. Okada, W. Cohen, A. Beaton, Jr., and C. Wisler, "A Study of the Achievement of Our Nation's Students," Washington, D.C.: U.S. Government Printing Office, 1973.

[41] Alvin Y. So and K.S. Chan, "What Matters? A Study of the Relative Impact of Language Background and Socioeconomic Status on Reading Achievement," Los Alamitos, CA: National Center for Bilingual Research, 1982; Calvin J. Veltman, "Relative Educational Attainment of Hispanic-American Children, 1976," *Metas* (1981), 2: 36-51; Edward A. De Avila, "Relative Language Proficiency Types: A Comparison of Prevalence, Achievement Level and Socioeconomic Status," report submitted to the Rand Corporation, Santa Monica, CA, 1980.

[42] Malcolm N. Danoff, Gary J. Coles, Donald H. McLaughlin, and Dorothy J. Reynolds, "Evaluation of the Impact of ESEA Title VII, Spanish/English Bilingual Education Program: Overview of Study and Findings," Palo Alto, CA: American Institutes for Research (AIR), 1978.

[43] Inspector General, "Review of Federal Bilingual Education Programs in Texas," Washington, D.C.: U.S. Department of Education, 1982.

[44] Inspector General, 1982.

[45] Heidi Dulay and Marina Burt, "The Relative Proficiency of Limited English Proficient Students," in J. Alatis (ed.), *Georgetown University Roundtable on Language and Linguistics,* Washington, D.C.: Georgetown University, 1980.

[46] Sharon E. Duncan and Edward A. De Avila, "Relative Language Proficiency and Field Dependence/Independence," paper presented at the annual meeting of TESOL, Boston, 1979.

[47] Nancy L. Russell and Alba A. Ortiz, "Assessment of Pragmatic Skills of Kindergarten Limited English Proficient Children in a Dialogue Model of Communication," paper presented at the annual meeting of the American Educational Research Association, San Francisco, CA, 1989.

[48] Charles L. Glenn, "Equity and Bilingual Education in Boston," Bureau of Educational Equity, Massachusetts Department of Education, 1985. Glenn did not calculate an average across high schools, so we computed a weighted average of the percent in 6+ years in each high school weighted by the number in the program.

[49] Glenn does note than some students who had been in for 6+ years were fluent in English. He offers two alternative hypotheses for this but neither has to do with the biases of the exit criterion.

[50] C. Perlman and W. Rice, Jr., "A Normative Study of a Test of English Language Proficiency," paper presented at the annual meeting of the American Educational Research Association, San Francisco, CA, 1979.

[51] Michael O'Malley, "Children's English and Services Study: Language Minority Children with Limited English Proficiency in the U.S.," Rosslyn, VA: InterAmerica Associates, 1981.

[52] Robert E. Barnes, "The Size of the Eligible Language Minority Population," in Keith Baker and Adriana de Kanter (eds.), *Bilingual Education: A Reappraisal of Federal Policy,* Lexington, MA: D.C. Heath and Company, 1983.

[53] Robert Berdan, Alvin So, and Angel Sanchez, "Language Among the Cherokee, Patterns of Language Use in Northeastern Oklahoma, Part 1, The Preliminary Report," Los Alamitos, CA: National Center for Bilingual Research, 1982.

[54] U.S. Bureau of the Census, Data for the Office of Planning, Budget and Evaluation, Decision Resources, 1984 Analysis, Department of Education, Washington, D.C., 1984.

[55] P.W. Airasian, T. Kellaghan, G.F. Madaus, and J.J. Pedulla, "Proportion and direction of teacher rating changes of pupil's progress attributable to standardized test information," *Journal of Educational Psychology* (1977), 69: 702-709; C. F. Sharpley and E. Edgar, "Teachers' Ratings vs. Standardized Tests: an Empirical Investigation of Agreement between Two Indices of Achievement, *Psychology in the Schools* (1986). 23:106-111; H.W. Stevenson, T. Parker, A. Wilkinson, A. Hegion, and E. Fish, "Predictive value of teachers' ratings of young children," *Journal of Educational Psychology* (1976), 68(5): 507-517.

[56] B.K. Keogh and L.D. Becker, "Early detection of learning problems: Questions, cautions, and guidelines," *Exceptional Children* (1973), 40:5-11; J. Tucker, "Issues and Considerations When Screening and Assessing Handicapped Pupils," *Measurement and Evaluation in Guidance* (1982), 15 (1):117-127.

[57] Betty J. Mace-Matluck, "A Longitudinal Study of the Oral Language Development of Texas Bilingual Children," paper presented at the National Conference on the Language Arts in the Elementary School, San Antonio, TX, 1980.

[58] S. Jackson, "Analysis Procedures and Summary Statistics of the Language Data of a Longitudinal Study of the Oral Language Development of Texas Bilingual Children," paper presented at the National Conference on the Language Arts in the Elementary School, San Antonio, TX, 1980.

[59] Russell and Ortiz, 1989:18.

[60] Southwest Regional Laboratories for Educational Research and Development (SWRL), "Development of Entry/Exit Criteria and Associated Assessment Procedures for Bilingual Education Projects", Los Alamitos, CA, 1981: 9.

CHAPTER SIX: THE COST OF TRANSITIONAL BILINGUAL EDUCATION

[1] Keith Baker was asked by the U.S. Department of Education to design a study that would give a reasonably accurate estimate of the cost of bilingual education programs. After looking into what such a study would require, he reported back to the management of the Department of Education that a minimal study would cost at least $2 million. Management decided they didn't want to know the cost of bilingual education that badly.

[2] 603 CMR, 14.05.

[3] The cost of the regular classroom program cannot be found by dividing the total school budget by the number of students (per-pupil cost) because this figure includes the cost of special programs, including bilingual education, as well as the cost of the regular classroom instructional program. It may take a lot of work to find the cost of the regular classroom program.

[4] American Legislative Exchange Council (ALEC) and U.S. English Foundation, *Bilingual Education in the United States 1991-92, Special Supplement, The Report Card on American Education,* 1994:3.

[5] These data come from the Special Issues Analysis Center under contract to the U.S. Department of Education.

[6] Massachusetts Department of Education, 1992-93 Preliminary Per Pupil Expenditures by Program.

[7] Margaret Carpenter-Huffman and Marta K. Salumon, "Case Studies of Delivery and Cost of Bilingual Education," prepared for the US Department of Education, 1981; Margaret Carpenter-Huffman and Marta K. Salumon, "Case Studies of Delivery and Cost of Bilingual Education," in Keith Baker and Adriana de Kanter (eds.), *Bilingual Education,* Lexington, MA: Lexington Books, 1983.

[8] These cost analyses are probably the best documentation available on what actually goes on in classrooms since having to measure all the costs forces the researcher to report the practices.

[9] J.A. Cardenas, J.J. Bernal, and W. Kean, "Bilingual Education Cost Analysis," San Antonio, TX: Intercultural Development Research Association, 1976; J.A. Cardenas, J.J. Bernal, and W. Kean, "Bilingual Education Cost Analysis: A Summary," San Antonio, TX: Intercultural Development Research Association, 1976.

[10] S.O. Garcia, "Analyzing Bilingual Education Costs," in G. Blanco et al. (ed.), *Bilingual Education: Current Perspectives,* Arlington, VA: Center for Applied Linguistics, 1978.

[11] Cynthia D. Prince and John A. Hubert, "Measuring the Cost of Bilingual Education," paper presented at the annual meeting of the American Educational Research Association, Boston, Massachusetts, 1990.

[12] Some school districts are dropped from the table because of missing data on one or another variable. South Middlesex Vocation Technical District reported no bilingual expenditure data to the state, although it has students in TBE, and so is dropped from this list. Bellingham reported $12,235 in per-pupil expenditures for bilingual education, but state reports show only three LEP students, none of them in TBE for that year. Ipswich reported $6,932 per-pupil expenditures for bilingual education, but state reports show only eight LEP students, none of them in TBE. Lenox reported $14,582 per-pupil expenditures for bilingual education, but state reports for that year show only two LEP students, and neither is in bilingual education. Millis reported a whopping $31,060 per pupil expenditures for bilingual education, but state reports show only two LEP students and neither is in bilingual education. Sharon reported $445 for bilingual education, but state reports show no LEP students and no TBE students. These six school districts were thus dropped from table 6-1.

[13] Indeed, over time the salary costs of the two programs will equalize. As the older group of regular classroom teachers ages and retires, they will be replaced with new younger teachers who are paid less than the bilingual education program teachers, reversing the initial apparent, but false, salary advantage for the bilingual education program.

[14] The English-speaking students enrolled in the bilingual education program are counted in the bilingual education program enrollment.

[15] Note that the full cost of teacher's salaries for this time is a program cost.

[16] Note that the average salary of school district employees carried on the school's books as teachers should not be used because many persons classified as teachers for payroll purposes are not classroom teachers.

[17] Sue Harget, "The Sustaining Effects Study," Santa Monica, CA: Systems Development Corporation, 1978.

[18] The added cost of TBE is calculated as follows. TBE = average teacher salary divided by the number of students in TBE - average teacher salary divided by number of students in the regular classroom. The added cost of ESL pullout for 1/6 of an instructional day = 1/6 (average teacher salary divided by ESL class size) - 1/6 (average teacher salary divided by regular class size) + average teacher salary divided by regular class size. If there are no salary differentials required by the program, teacher salaries will be the same in each calculation, and with a class size of 18, the TBE program will cost less than a regular classroom of 31 with a nine student pullout program.

CHAPTER SEVEN: OPINION SURVEYS

[1] Parents of LEP children could be interviewed by means of random digit dialing, but the cost of that for a sample of 200 Spanish, 200 Portuguese, and 200 Cambodian students was more than $80,000 because of all the "dead-end" interviewing that would be needed. Ninety-five percent or more of the individuals called would not be parents of LEP children, but we would not know this until we asked several screening questions.

[2] Joan Baratz-Snowden, Donald Rock, Judith Pollack, and Gita Wilder, "Parent Preference Study," Princeton, N.J.: Educational Testing Service, 1988. Keith Baker was the project manager of the ETS study for the U.S. Department of Education.

[3] *Roper Reports,* June 1982.

[4] Gallup Organization, January 10, 1991.

[5] Christine Rossell designed the survey. It was carried out and reported by Thomas E. Whalen. “Berkeley Unified School District, Bilingual Education Parent Survey, Spring 1988,” Hayward, CA: California State University, 1988.

[6] D. Cardoza, A. Sanchez, and R. Mendoza, "Attitudes Toward Bilingual Education and Foreign Language Instruction Among Four Ethnolinguistic Groups," Los Alamitos, CA: National Center for Bilingual Research, 1985.

[7] Neither the mean for both Hispanic groups nor the mean for both Asian groups is shown in Cardoza, Sanchez, and Mendoza. We provide a weighted mean (response times N for each group divided by the total N for Hispanics or Asians) that we calculated from the information in their tables.

[8] Huddy and Sears (1990) classified as "substantially accurate" the following: "teaching foreign students in their own language"; "teaching in two languages"; and “teaching English to foreign students." This amounted to 31 percent of the population. We disagree with their classification of "teaching English to foreign students" as a substantially accurate representation of bilingual education. To our mind, this is not a unique charac-

teristic of bilingual education nor is it what makes it controversial. "Teaching English to foreign students" could as easily refer to ESL or structured immersion as to bilingual education. Therefore, we count only the first two categories—"teaching foreign students in their own language" and "teaching in two languages"—as substantially accurate, reducing the percentage of accurate descriptions to 22 percent. Leonie Huddy and David O. Sears, "Qualified Public Support for Bilingual Education: Some Policy Implications," *The Annals of the American Academy of Political and Social Science* (March 1990) 508: 119-134.

[9] Kenji Hakuta, "Bilingual Education in the Public Eye: A Case Study of New Haven, Connecticut," *NABE Journal* (1984), 9:53-76.

[10] We calculated this as follows: If respondents had seen these two options as mutually exclusive, 24 percent of the respondents would have said maintaining Spanish should be emphasized because this is the percentage that said entering an English-only class as quickly as possible should *not* be emphasized. Instead, 58 percent said Spanish should be maintained. The difference between 58 and 24 percent is 34 percent—the minimum percentage of respondents who must have answered yes to both English-only and Spanish maintenance.

[11] Baratz-Snowden et al., 1988.

[12] Questions marked with an asterisk are not from the ETS report, but from our reanalysis of the survey data.

[13] These parents probably overestimated their child's English language ability since they probably were not discerning critics of a language in which they themselves were not very proficient. It should be noted that only 34 percent of Mexican-American and 32 percent of Asian parents rated their child's *native tongue* ability as pretty good or very good, suggesting that when parents were proficient in the language being discussed they were more discerning.

[14] Ramirez et al. (1991), Rossell (1992), and Burkheimer et al. (1989) document in detail exactly how much less instruction in English, math, and other subjects students receive who are enrolled in a bilingual education program with native tongue instruction. The Ramirez et al. study demonstrated (see also Rossell, 1992:169) that there was 25 to 35 percent less English in grades K to 2 in both the TBE and bilingual maintenance programs than in the immersion program. In grade 3, the disparity was reduced to 18 to 23 percent less English in the bilingual programs. In grade 4, the TBE program had about the same percentage of English as the structured immersion program, but the bilingual maintenance program still had 10 percent less. There was also about 5 percent less math in the bilingual programs from kindergarten through grade 4. Every analyst who has looked carefully at what goes on in the classrooms documents that including Spanish in the curriculum of the public school reduces the amount of

English language instructional time, as well as time spent on other subjects since the school day is not extended. J. Ramirez, S. Yuen, D. Ramey, and D. Pasta, *Final Report: Longitudinal Study of Structured English Immersion Strategy, Early-Exit and Late-Exit Transitional Bilingual Education Programs for Language-Minority Children,* Vol. I, prepared for U.S. Department of Education, San Mateo, CA: Aguirre International, 1991; J. Ramirez, D. Pasta, S. Yuen, D. Billings, and D. Ramey, *Final Report: Longitudinal Study of Structured English Immersion Strategy, Early-Exit and Late-Exit Transitional Bilingual Education Programs for Language-Minority Children,* Vol. II, prepared for U.S. Department of Education, San Mateo, CA: Aguirre International, 1991; Christine Rossell, "Nothing Matters? A Critique of the Ramirez et al. Longitudinal Study of Instructional Programs for Language-Minority Children," *Bilingual Research Journal* (1992), 16 (1&2):159-186; G.J. Burkheimer, A. Conger, G. Dunteman, B. Elliott, and K. Mowbray, *Effectiveness of services for language minority limited English proficient students,* Raleigh-Durham, NC: Research Triangle Institute, 1989.

[15] Although one survey (Cardoza, Sanchez, and Mendoza, 1985) showed differences between Japanese and Chinese parents in support for bilingual education, the differences between these two groups were less than the differences between Asians as a group and Hispanics as a group. In addition, the Japanese are such a small percentage of Asian immigrants (1.5 percent as of the 1990 census) that even if they had very different attitudes from others, it would have little influence on survey results for Asians.

CHAPTER EIGHT: WHAT WE HAVE FOUND AND WHAT MUST BE DONE

[1] Seventy-one percent of Spanish LEP students and 62 percent of the other LEP students are in grades K-6; this amounts to two students per grade at the elementary level and one per grade in high school.

[2] One of the two main mistakes of the Ramirez et al. 1991 study was the use of nominal program designation—early-exit TBE, late-exit TBE, and structured immersion—as the treatment variable rather than the percentage of English used in instruction, which varied considerably within nominal program categories and by subject matter. The second mistake, as mentioned in chapter 3, was the failure to directly compare with statistical analyses the late-exit program to the early-exit and immersion programs. See Christine Rossell, "Nothing Matters? A Critique of the Ramírez, et al. Longitudinal Study of Instructional Programs for Language-Minority Children," *Bilingual Research Journal* (1992), 16 (1&2):159-186; Keith Baker, "Ramírez et al.: Led by Bad Theory," *Bilingual Research Journal* (1992), 16 (1&2):91-104; and

M. Meyer and S. Fienberg (eds.), *Assessing Evaluation Studies: The case of bilingual education strategies,* Washington, D.C.: National Academy Press, 1992.

[3] When we inform intellectuals outside the education field who have never heard of the theory behind bilingual education, they think we are joking. The most common response is, "Doesn't everyone know that the best way to learn a language is to be immersed in it?" Bilingual education is practiced all over the world, but the theory used in the United States is almost unknown outside this country. When we inform educators from other countries that have bilingual education of the theory behind bilingual education as it is practiced in this country, the most common response is, "Doesn't everyone know that the only purpose of bilingual education is to enable students to retain their native tongue?"

[4] See, for example, F.B. Moore and G.D. Parr, "Models of bilingual education: Comparisons of effectiveness," *The Elementary School Journal* (1978), 79:93-97; Christine Rossell, "The Effectiveness of Educational Alternatives for Limited-English-Proficient Children," in *Learning in Two Languages,* New Brunswick: Transaction Publishers, 1990; Rossell, 1991.

[5] The procedures currently used consistently overidentify students as LEP. Knowing this, researchers should take special care to determine those who are truly LEP. One way to do this is to assume that any kindergarten student who is able to take a preliterate test like the TOBE in English is potentially FEP regardless of any later score on the CTBS. The teacher's rating of each individual student's proficiency in English should be a factor since research shows that teachers are the equal of foreign language experts and are better judges of a student's English language proficiency than are standardized tests. In addition, one could compare a student's Spanish language proficiency and English language proficiency. Those who score lower in Spanish than in English are potentially FEP regardless of their English language score. In addition to these criteria, students classified as LEP could be divided into those who score within a few points of the cut-off score for classification and those who score significantly lower. None of these criteria by itself is fool-proof, but taken collectively they might be able to distinguish children who are truly LEP when they enter these programs from those who are probably FEP, but for various reasons are classified as LEP. See Christine Rossell and Keith Baker, "Selecting and exiting students in bilingual education programs," *Journal of Law and Education* (1988), 17 (4):589-623.

[6] See G.J. Burkheimer, Jr., A. Conger, G. Dunteman, B. Elliott, and K. Mowbray, "Effectiveness of services for language minority limited English proficient students," Raleigh-Durham, NC.: Research Triangle Institute, 1989.

[7] McCarthy and Valdez (1986) analyzed census data of Mexican-American immigrants in California and found that 90 percent of first generation native born Mexican-Americans are bilingual and fluent in English. Twenty-five percent are English monolingual. Among the second generation, virtually all are fluent in English, and more than half are monolingual English. Thus, Mexican-Americans acquire English and lose their native tongue like every other immigrant group. Kevin F. McCarthy and R. Burciaga Valdez, "Current and Future Effects of Mexican Immigration in California," Santa Monica, CA: The Rand Corporation, 1986.

[8] Lindholm and Fairchild (1990) and Bamford and Mizokawa (1992) found a small negative effect on students English language development, and McCollum (1993) found some negative attitudes among students in a two-way program toward Spanish in comparison to English. Kathryn J. Lindholm and Halford H. Fairchild, "Evaluation of an Elementary School Bilingual Immersion Program," in A. Padilla et al. (eds.), *Bilingual Education: Issues and Strategies,* Newbury Park, CA: Sage Publications, 1990; Kathryn W. Bamford and Donald T. Mizokawa, "Spanish Immersion Children in Washington State: Fourth Year of a Longitudinal Study," paper presented at the annual meeting of the American Educational Research Association, San Francisco, 1992; Pamela A. McCollum, "Learning to Value English: Cultural Capital in a Two-Way Bilingual Program," paper presented at the annual meeting of the American Educational Research Association, Atlanta, Georgia, 1993.

On the other hand, Lambert's 1992 evaluation of the Cambridge Amigos K-3 program shows a small deficit in English for English speakers that is not statistically significant, and it does show an improvement in attitudes and friendship choices. "Interim Progress Report: The Amigos Program Evaluation Grade K Through 3: 1990-1991," working paper, 1992.

The Thomas and Collier (95) research project, about which there has been some publicity, is not discussed here primarily because it is not finished—what has been distributed to reporters and the public so far is a three-page summary titled "Research Summary of Study in Progress" with two pages of graphs and very little information. Moreover, they appear to have made a serious error in the analysis shown in the graphs since "language minority" (not LEP) children in two-way bilingual education are 30 points above TBE students. No one in the history of bilingual education research or educational research in general for that matter has seen such differences in such similar programs when matching of groups is properly done. One can only wonder why they disseminated their "study in progress" findings without checking their data.

[9] The school district did agree to stop its 20-year practice of testing students on the basis of Hispanic surname alone for a probationary period.

"NYC to Stop Proficiency Testing of All Hispanics," *Education Week,* 3 March 1996.

Index

A

B

C

T

U

Y

About the Authors

Christine H. Rossell, Ph.D., is a professor of political science at Boston University and former chair of the political science department. She has written extensively on bilingual education and school desegregation.

Keith Baker, Ph.D., is a private social science research consultant living in Silver Springs, Maryland. He has worked at the U.S. Department of Education and has taught at Pennsylvania State University.

Pioneer Publications in Print

Pioneer Paper No. 1, *The Massachusetts Health Plan: The Right Prescription* by Attiat Ott and Wayne B. Gray, 1988 out of print—photocopy available.

Pioneer Paper No. 2, *The Cost of Regulated Pricing: A Critical Analysis of Auto Insurance Premium Rate Setting in Massachusetts* by Simon Rottenberg, 1989 out of print—photocopy available.

Pioneer Paper No. 3, *Work and Welfare in Massachusetts: An Evaluation of the ET Program* by June O'Neill, 1990.

Pioneer Paper No. 4, *Mental Retardation Programs: How Does Massachusetts Compare?* by Edward Moscovitch, 1990.

Pioneer Paper No. 5, *School Choice in Massachusetts* by Abigail Thernstrom, 1991.

Pioneer Paper No. 6, *By Choice or By Chance? Tracking Values in Massachusetts' Public Spending* by Herman B. Leonard, 1992.

Pioneer Paper No. 7, *Reinventing the Schools: A Radical Plan for Boston* by Steven F. Wilson, 1992.

Pioneer Paper No. 8, *Special Education: Good Intentions Gone Awry* by Edward Moscovitch, 1994.

Pioneer Paper No. 9, *Agenda For Leadership* edited by James A. Peyser, 1994.

Pioneer Paper No. 10, *Bilingual Education: The Emperor Has No Clothes* by Christine Rossell and Keith Baker, 1996.

Forthcoming from Pioneer:

Workers' Compensation in Massachusetts, by James Chelius and Edward Moscovitch, estimated publication date, August, 1996.

Economic Development Policies, by Edwin Mills, estimated publication date, November, 1996.